Albert Alonzo Lovell

Worcester in the War of the Revolution

Embracing the Acts of the Town from 1765 to 1783 Inclusive

Albert Alonzo Lovell

Worcester in the War of the Revolution
Embracing the Acts of the Town from 1765 to 1783 Inclusive

ISBN/EAN: 9783337116330

Printed in Europe, USA, Canada, Australia, Japan

Cover: Foto ©ninafisch / pixelio.de

More available books at **www.hansebooks.com**

THE MEETING HOUSE, (OLD SOUTH,) 1763,
And as it appeared in 1776.

WORCESTER

IN THE

WAR OF THE REVOLUTION;

EMBRACING THE

ACTS OF THE TOWN

FROM 1765 TO 1783 INCLUSIVE.

WITH AN

APPENDIX.

By ALBERT A. LOVELL.

WORCESTER, MASS.:
PRINTED BY TYLER & SEAGRAVE, 442 MAIN STREET,
Spy Building, opposite City Hall.
1876.

PREFACE.

Perhaps it is unnecessary for the writer to state that this is an unpretentious work. He has endeavored to tell the story of Worcester in the Revolution, as much as possible, in the language of the men and documents of that time. He is well aware that some of the facts narrated have become twice told tales, but he flatters himself that by far the greater portion, which has heretofore lain buried in dusty nooks and corners, is now published for the first time.

In these busy times, when the thoughts and energies of the people are directed in so great a degree to the pursuit of wealth, comfort and enjoyment, it cannot be otherwise than profitable to pause and look back upon the acts of those whose wisdom, foresight and self-denial, laid the foundations of that prosperity which we their descendants enjoy—to spend a while with them and catch the inspiration of liberty and freedom from a contemplation of their sacrifices and sufferings—that we be not degenerate sons of worthy sires.

There is much material accessible for an exhaustive history of Worcester during this period of its existence, some of which is carefully preserved, some hidden in the rubbish of garrets and closets, soon to find its way to market at a pittance per pound; and other still floating down through the closing years of a century in tradition, soon to be lost in distance, and buried in oblivion.

Worcester has a revolutionary history to which her sons may point with pride; and "by honoring the parent, the child honors himself."

The work of collecting and compiling, was entered into by the author through a natural taste for the gathering of memorials of the past, without the most distant thought of publishing any of the results of his labors; but with a feeling, that at the close of a century of the nation's life, when our thoughts naturally revert to the days of its birth, those who shall honor him by a perusal of these pages will overlook all shortcomings and demerits, he has yielded to solicitation, and presents this volume to a forbearing public.

He takes great pleasure in expressing his obligations to Mr. Samuel F. Haven, Librarian of the American Antiquarian Society, Mr. Edmund M. Barton, Assistant Librarian, Mr. Daniel Seagrave, Rev. George Allen, Mr. Samuel Smith, City Clerk, and others, for many favors received at their hands.

WORCESTER, May 15, 1876.

TABLE OF CONTENTS.

CHAPTER I.
Page.

Worcester at breaking out of the Revolutionary War—Population—Valuation—Means of postal communication—General aspect of town—Roads—Gallows and Stocks—Notices of eminent men and their residences—Common and burial ground—The Old South Meeting house,   9

CHAPTER II.

State of Public opinion previous to the war—Instructions to the Representative to the General Court concerning the Stamp Act in 1765, and against slavery in 1767—Agreement not to buy or use any article that had paid a duty, 1768—Committee of Correspondence chosen in 1773—Formation of the American Political Society in 1773, together with its proceedings up to its dissolution in 1776—Action of the Town on the Tea Act, 1774—Protest of the Tories to this action—Instruction to Representative concerning the Tea question—New Town Meeting called by the Tories to reconsider instructions—Great battle at the Polls and victory of the Patriots—Long protest of the Tories clandestinely entered on records of Town—Town Clerk obliged to expunge the same in open meeting, by dipping his fingers in ink and drawing them over the page—Recantation of 43 of the 52 Tories,   17

CHAPTER III.

The Port Bill—The Mandamus Councillors—Preparation for armed resistance—Court suspended—Recantation of Mr. Campbell—Instruction to Representative to General Court and Delegate to Provincial Congress—Action of the Committee of Safety concerning Supplies, Arms, Ammunition, &c.,—Drilling of the Minute Men—Call "to arms!" "to arms!" April 19, 1775—March to Boston—Press of Isaiah Thomas removed to Worcester—Letter of John Hancock to Committee of Safety—Tories severely looked after—Worcester men at Bunker Hill—Instruction to Delegate to Provincial Congress—Dr. Willard's Recantation, - - - - - - - - - - - - 43

CHAPTER IV.

Col. Ward's Regiment petition the General Assembly concerning the tories—The tories address Gen. Gage on his departure for England—Clark Chandler committed to jail for assisting a prisoner of war to escape—He petitions the General Court and Committee of Safety for enlargement—Town voted to sustain the measure if Congress should declare the American Colonies independent—Troops armed and forwarded to Boston, New York and Canada—The price of Bohea Tea and other articles fixed by Congress, - - - - - - - 68

CHAPTER V.

Declaration of Independence—Subsequent celebration of the event—Calls for more troops promptly met—New York sends its tories to Worcester jail—Address of Committee of Correspondence recommending milder measures concerning suspected persons—One-seventh male inhabitants drafted—Escape and capture of a portion of the New York captives—Town excited because of change of basis of Representation to General Court—Bounty voted to recruits—Money raised by general tax—Tories prosecuted—Soldiers march to the relief of Northern Army—Another draft—A company march to oppose Burgoyne—Burgoyne's captive army pass through town—Town voted to approve of Confederation of States—Town voted not to approve Constitution recomended for State—Banishment and confiscation of the property of certain tories, - - - - - - - - - - - - - 81

CHAPTER VI.

Convention to consider the question of Finance—Action of the town thereon—County Convention for the same purpose and its proceedings, fixing prices of labor and produce—Delegates elected to a Constitutional Convention—Further requisition for men and means answered—Bill of Rights and Constitution accepted, with some exceptions—First election under the Constitution—More men and provisions supplied for the army—Worcester thinks she has contributed more money and men than her proportion—Surrender of Cornwallis—Jubilation—Instructions to Representative on grievances, - - - - - 94

CHAPTER VII.

Slavery abolished by decision of the Court at Worcester—Treaty of Peace —Celebration—The question of absentees and refugees considered, 105

APPENDIX.

Town Officers from 1774 to 1783,	115
Jury List for 1776,	117
List of Voters, 1775,	118
Roll of Capt. Timothy Bigelow's Company of Minute men,	119
Roll of Benjamin Flagg's Company of Minute men,	120
Roll of men from Worcester under Capt. Jonas Hubbard,	120
List of men in Col. Thomas Craft's Regiment of Artillery, 1775,	121
Men from Worcester in other Companies, 1775,	121
Roll of Capt. William Gates' Company, 1776,	121
Men from Worcester in Col. Thomas Craft's Regiment of Artillery, 1776,	122
List of men in Col. Thomas Craft's Regiment of Artillery, 1777,	122
Roll of Capt. David Chadwick's Company, 1777,	123
Nine Months' men, 1778,	123
Men from Worcester in Continental Service, 1778,	124
Nine Months' men, drafted in 1779,	124
List of Six Months' men—Resolve of June, 1780,	124
List of men from Worcester, 1780—Returned Dec. 27, 1781,	124
Six Months' men from Worcester, 1780,	124
Memorandum from Army Books, 1780,	125
Memorandum from Army Books in Land Office,	125
Quaint Advertizements of the Period,	126
Prices of Pews in Meeting House, 1763,	128

CHAPTER I.

Worcester at breaking out of the Revolutionary War—Population—Valuation—Means of postal communication—General aspect of town—Roads—Gallows and Stocks—Notices of eminent men and their residences—Common and burial ground—The Old South Meeting house.

It would be desirable, if it were possible, to present a full and detailed representation of Worcester as it was at the time of the Revolution, but as the records of that day are meagre, and we so far removed in point of time, it is impossible to produce any full and complete picture of the town at that period of its existence.

At the breaking out of the war in 1775, Worcester contained about nineteen hundred inhabitants. According to a census taken in the year 1763, the population was fourteen hundred and seventy-eight, and by a census taken in the year 1776, it was found to be nineteen hundred and twenty-five, an increase in thirteen years of four hundred and forty-seven, or nearly thirty-one per cent. In 1790 the population was ascertained to be two thousand and ninety-five, an increase in fourteen years of nearly nine per cent.

As to valuation, we find by the list for the year 1772, the town ranked fourth in the County, being exceeded by Lancaster, Brookfield and Sutton. According to the list of 1778 it then ranked third, Brookfield occupying the first place on the list and Lancaster the second. From the returns of the Assessors in the office of the Secretary of State, the following estimate of the principal articles of property for the year 1781 is obtained, viz: houses 216, barns 207, shops 11, other buildings 32. Live Stock—cows and steers 778, horses 277, oxen 365, swine 212. Land—tillage 1034 acres, mowing 1074, meadow 1606, pasture 2881, woodland and unimproved 14,912.

The means of communication between Worcester and the other parts of the Province previous to the war and during its continuance were very limited. In 1774, the only regular communication was by a post going once a week between Boston and Hartford, occupying six days in the journey. On the establishment of the Spy in the town in 1775 by Mr. Thomas, he made extensive arrangements for its distribution, sending post riders to Cambridge, Salem, Providence, Fitchburg and other places. The roads were poor and almost all travelling was performed on horseback. On the 15th of November, 1775, the first post office of the town was established, Mr. Isaiah Thomas being postmaster.[*]

Perhaps in no way can a clearer idea of the general aspect of the town at that time be obtained, than by commencing at the northerly end of the village on the Boston road, and following that and the main road to a point just south of the meeting house, taking note of the more prominent land-marks. About a quarter of a mile above what is now known as Lincoln Square, on the Boston road, on the west side, stood the residence of the Hon. Timothy Paine, for many years a member of the General Court, and a stout government man in the controversies in that body during the years which preceded the Revolution. Near the residence of Mr. Paine a short distance below was the house of Levi Lincoln, Sen., afterwards Governor of the State and Attorney General of the United States under President Jefferson.

---

[*] Lincoln's History of Worcester.

The grounds connected with this estate were considered the finest in the town. Still farther down, stood the Hancock Arms Tavern, the principal rendezvous of the patriots. At this house most of the people in attendance at the courts were accustomed to stop. It was formerly owned by the Hon. John Hancock, and here he usually spent a portion of the summer after the courts had adjourned, and entertained his friends. South of this tavern stood the jail built in 1753. This jail was during the war crowded with prisoners from the British army and tories from this and the other Provinces. On the north side of the present Lincoln Square was the Salisbury Mansion erected in 1770. This house is still standing, and is almost the only remaining relic of those days which preserves a semblance of its original appearance. It has been remodelled to some extent, and raised so that it stands a few feet higher than when built. As originally constructed it provided a commodious residence for Mr. Stephen Salisbury and his mother, while a portion was fitted for and occupied as a store, where he carried on an extensive business, after having abandoned the one which stood on the site now covered by the Worcester & Nashua Railroad Station. On the south side of the Square was the blacksmith shop of Timothy Bigelow.

The only roads converging at this point at that time were the Boston road, now Lincoln street, the road now known as Salisbury street, the road which is now Summer street, and the main road of the village. On the west side of the main road, on the elevation occupied at the present day by the Court Houses, stood the Court House of that day, erected in 1751, a wooden building 36 feet by 40 in size. It was afterwards removed to make room for a building furnishing larger accommodations, and now stands at the intersection of Franklin and Green streets.

The main road, as it left what is now the Square, was very narrow, the bank on the west side extending much farther east than at present. The road to the Court House left the main road near where the Central Church now stands, and terminated at the Court House, although there was a path down the hill toward the Salisbury Mansion, in the rear of a store which stood near where the bank wall now terminates. In front of the Court House was the pillory, whipping post and gallows. This gallows was not used for executions but for the punishment of those guilty of minor crimes, the culprit being compelled to sit with a rope around his neck in view of passers by. The stocks were located near the meeting house, (the Old South,) and stored in that building when not in use.

Nearly opposite where School street now enters Main, was the store of Dr. Elijah Dix, where as physician and druggist, he maintained an extensive practice and thriving business. To this man are we of the present generation greatly indebted for the magnificent elms which grace our principal street, he planting many himself and inducing others to do the same.

At the foot of the present George street lived Mr. Nathan Baldwin. The house which he occupied is still standing on its original site, and now presents the same general appearance as when built. Mr. Baldwin was a master spirit of the patriotic party in Worcester. He was an able writer, and the author of most of the public documents issued by the town and Committee of Correspondence. In his religious views he was a Deist; and John Adams, afterwards President, speaks in one of his letters of Nathan Baldwin as one of three notable disputants in a religious controversy which raged in town when he came here to live in 1755.

On the opposite side of the road, on land occupied at the present day by the Bay State House, was the Heywood Tavern, owned at this time by Daniel Heywood, a young man under age, to whom it was bequeathed by his grandfather, Dea. Daniel Heywood. Upon the incorporation of Worcester County in 1731, a chamber in this house was fitted up and used for a jail until the County provided a building for that purpose.

Farther south, on the west side, where the Lincoln House now stands, stood the King's Arms Tavern, kept by the widow Mary Sternes. It was, in the early days of the war the tory head-quarters, and the place where most of the schemes for defeating the purposes of the patriots were devised. In front of this tavern was a sign post on which swung the sign of the King's Arms, but which was taken down and burned at the first celebration of the Declaration of Independence in this town in 1776.

On the opposite side, where Clark's block now stands, was the Sun Tavern, and in front a swinging sign on which were represented the setting sun and a dying oak. Next south of this tavern stood the house of Col. John Chandler, for many years Town Clerk and a strong sympathizer with the British Government, and adjoining was the store of that gentleman, located on what is now the corner of Main and Front streets. This building—" the Old Compound"—was removed about twenty-five years since.

Just south of the junction of the Hardwick road, now Pleasant street, with the main road, stood a fine elm, one of the largest in the town; and standing back some distance, with a large unenclosed yard in front, was the house of John Nazro, a prominent merchant. This house was formerly the residence of Rev. Isaac Burr, Pastor of the Parish from 1725 to 1745. Precisely opposite the present City Hall was situated Mr. Nazro's store.

On the Hardwick road, where High street now joins Pleasant, stood a small red house which was occupied by Mr. Isaiah Thomas after his arrival in Worcester.

On what is now Front street situated between the present Salem and Trumbull streets, was the house of Capt. Palmer Goulding, a prominent citizen, and for some years Town Clerk.

On the spot now occupied by the new Union Depot, where at that time was a sandy knoll, took place in the year 1778, one of the most remarkable executions for capital crime which ever occurred in this country. Four malefactors, one of whom was a woman, were here executed for the crime of murder. About five thousand people from this, and neighboring towns, thronged to witness the spectacle. A terrible thunder shower occurred at the time, and everything conspired to produce " a compound scene of horror." The details were published in the Spy of Aug. 6, 1778.

Returning to the Main road, south of the store of Mr. Nazro, on the site now occupied by Taylor's block, was the residence of Col. Gardner Chandler, High Sheriff of the County. This house was considered one of the finest in the interior of New England. Near the present junction of Portland and Park streets, stood the house of Rev. Thaddeus Maccarty, pastor of the Parish. At the point where Park street now joins Main, stood the residence of James Putnam, Esq., the able lawyer and the last Royal Attorney General of the Province. After Col. Putnam fled to Boston, the house was occupied by Joseph Allen, Esq., and still later by Mr. Samuel Flagg. It was destroyed by fire in 1786. Just south of this house was Jones' Tavern, another rendezvous of the tories.

The territory lying between the store of Col. Chandler on the north-west, the house of Palmer Goulding on the east, the houses of Rev. Mr. Maccarty and Col. Putnam on the south, and the main road on the west, was the Common, on the east side of which was the public burial place of the town, surrounded by a high stone wall. The Common at that day was not enclosed, and was used as a common in the most literal sense. Travelled ways, some of which had been established by the authority of the town, and some by use, traversed this tract in all directions. On the west side near the main road, on the same site it now occupies, stood the meeting house built in 1763. The original dimensions were 70 feet in length by 55 in width, with a tower on the north surmounted by a spire 130 feet high. The erection of this building was commenced June 21, 1763, and although not fully completed, the first public service was held Dec. 8, of that year, that being the day set apart for Thanksgiving in this Province. The principal entrance was through a porch on the west side, and there was also an entrance through a porch at the south end, and another through the tower on the north. The porch at the main entrance had wide double doors in front and single doors at the sides. The entrance through the tower was also by doors on the three sides. The floor of the meeting house was provided with sixty-one large square box pews* and seven long pews on each side of the broad aisle,—these last being free. Those at the right on entering were assigned to the men, and those on the left to the women. In front of the pulpit was the pew for the deacons, and the pew for the aged and

---

*See Appendix page 128.

deaf. Over the pulpit was the high sounding board with its pendant dove. On three sides was a very deep gallery, the pulpit being raised high enough to be in full view of every seat. The pew at the right of the pulpit on the floor of the house, was assigned to the Hon. John Chandler, as being the most desirable, in acknowledgment of his generous contribution of £40 towards the erection of the edifice. The building committee consisted of John Chandler, Jr., Joshua Bigelow, Josiah Brewer, John Curtis, James Putnam, Daniel Boyden, James Goodwin, Jacob Hemmenway, David Bigelow, Samuel Moore, and Elisha Smith. They were originally limited by the town to an expenditure of £1200, but the entire expense amounted to £1542. No change took place in the exterior until the year 1827, when the west porch was removed, wings added to the tower, and various minor alterations made. In 1834, the south porch was removed and 25 feet in length added to the building; the addition preserving the general style of architecture as it was at the time the church was first erected. In 1871, the outside was modernized, five long windows being substituted on each side in place of the eighteen which had lighted the building before, leaving but little to remind us of its former ap- pearance.

Having taken this hasty glance at Worcester as it was at the time of the Revolution, we can realize, to some extent, the changes of a century. A small town of less than two thousand inhabitants has become a thriving city of nearly fifty thousand, with a total valuation of forty-nine millions of dollars. Its village highway is to-day a busy thoroughfare, and scarcely aught remains of one hundred years ago.

Plan of the Lower Floor of the Meeting-House, 1763.

No 21 Robert Barker	No 20 Rhoba and Robert Smith.	No 19 Daniel and Alel Heywood	No 18 John Chandler, Esq.	PULPIT	No 17 Jacob Hemenway	No 16 Francis Harrington	No 15 Josiah Harrington	No 14 Daniel Ward	No 13 Tyrus Rice
No 22 Jacob Chamberlin	No 48 James McFarland	No 49 Daniel McFarland	No 50 Town's Pew	Seat for the Aged and Deaf					No 12 Joshua Whitney
				Deacon's Seat	No 45 James Putnam Esq	No 46 Gershom and Comfort Rice	No 47 Jonathan Snow		
No 23 Phebe Smith, jr									No 11 Nath'l Moore
No 24 Isaac Greason	No 51 John Curtis						No 44 Thos. Prentice		No 10 Nathan Perry
No 25 Samuel Miller	No 52 Joseph Stearns, Esq						No 43 John Boyden		No 9 Joseph Clark Jr
South Entrance through the Tower	No 53 Luke Brown						No 42 Daniel Boyden		Entrance through South Porch
No 26 Joseph Pearce	No 54 William McFarland	No 55 Benj. Flagg	No 56 Mathew Gray	No 57 Isaac Heywood	No 38 Thomas Rice	No 39 John Chadwick	No 40 Daniel Pancroft	No 41 Samuel Curtis	No 8 James Nichols
No 27 Rachel Rice	No 58 Isaac Moore	No 59 Joseph Blair	No 60 Isaac A. Daniel Flint	No 61 Robert Gray, Jr	No 34 Clement Lovell	No 35 Asa Moore	No 36 John Mower	No 37 Thomas Palmer	No 7 John Chandler, Esq. Assignee of Asa Flagg
No 28 Samuel Hand, Assignee of Thomas Vardin									No 6 John Mahon
No 29 Israel Trowbton	No 30 Jacob Holmes	No 31 Samuel Mower	No 32 John Chandler, Esq	No 33 Timothy Palmer, Esq	Entrance by Front or West Porch	No 1 Nathaniel Adams	No 2 Gardner Chandler, Esq	No 3 James Brown	No 4 Thomas Wheeler	No 5 John Chandler, Esq

CHAPTER II.

State of Public opinion previous to the war—Instructions to the Representative to the General Court concerning the Stamp Act in 1765, and against slavery in 1767—Agreement not to buy or use any article that had paid a duty, 1768—Committee of Correspondence chosen in 1773—Formation of the American Political Society in 1773, together with its proceedings up to its dissolution in 1776—Action of the Town on the Tea Act, 1774—Protest of the Tories to this action—Instruction to Representative concerning the Tea question—New Town Meeting called by the Tories to reconsider instructions—Great battle at the Polls and Victory of the Patriots—Long protest of the Tories clandestinely entered on records of Town—Town Clerk obliged to expunge the same in open meeting, by dipping his fingers in ink and drawing them over the page—Recantation of 43 of the 52 Tories.

In taking a retrospective survey of the acts of the town and people of Worcester during the War of the Revolution, it will be necessary, in order to properly understand the bearing of the great questions with which they had to deal, the apparently insurmountable obstacles with which they had to contend, and, at the same time, to fully appreciate their undying attachment to those principles of liberty which finally gave birth to the republic, to review their acts and doings to some extent during the decade which preceded the final appeal to arms.

In this review we shall see they were loyal subjects of Great Britain, having been at all times ready to take up arms in defence of the mother country, and in thus defending her, were willing to peril both life and fortune. But while firmly loyal to King George and his Parliament, they could but realize that the chains of slavery were being forged for them, and unhesitatingly, yet calmly and reluctantly resolved, that loyal though they wished to be, that loyalty should not be maintained at the expense of the God-given right of freedom.

Going back ten years previous to the breaking out of hostilities, we find that at a town meeting held October 21, 1765, Capt. Ephraim Doolittle, Representative to the General Court, was instructed to join in no measure countenancing the Stamp Act. On the 18th of May, 1767, at a town meeting, a committee consisting of Capt. Ephraim Doolittle, Nathan Baldwin and Jonathan Stone reported instructions to be observed by Mr. Joshua Bigelow, Representative, as follows:

First: That you use your influence to maintain and continue that harmony and good will between Great Britain and this Province, which may be most conducive to the prosperity of each, by a steady and firm attachment to English liberty and the charter rights of this Province, and that you willingly suffer no invasions, either through pretext of precedency, or any other way whatsoever; and if you find any encroachments on our charter rights, that you use your utmost ability to obtain constitutional redress.

Second: That you use your influence to obtain a law to put an end to the unchristian and impolitic practice of making slaves of the human species.

Third: That you use your influence that the pay of sheriffs be so regulated that the fees may not be double as much as the service may be done for, and that jurymen be not obliged to do service at the expense of their own private estates, or be subjected to large fines or penalties.

Fourth: That you endeavor to relieve the people of the province of the great burden of supporting so many Latin schools, whereby they are prevented from attaining such a degree of English learning as is necessary to retain the freedom of any state.

Fifth: That you inquire into the cause of such general neglect of the militia of this Province.

Sixth: That you take special care of the liberty of the press, and in all matters to have a single eye to the public good, and a watchful eye over those who are seeking the ruin of this Province, and endeavor to make this Province reciprocally happy with our mother country.

In 1768 an agreement was signed by the patriotic people of the town to the effect, that "as the happiness and well being of civil communities depend upon industry, economy and good morals," and taking into consideration the stagnation of business, scarcity of money, and the heavy debt contracted in the French and Indian War, they would use their utmost endeavor in order to retain money in the Province, suppress extravagance and promote industry, economy and good morals, to discountenance the use of all foreign superfluities, and encourage the manufacturers of the Province; and they resolved, that as Parliament had passed an act imposing duties on various articles for the purpose of raising a revenue, which they regarded as an infringement on their just rights and privileges, they solemnly promised and engaged each with the other, to encourage our own manufacturers, to avoid paying the tax by not buying any European commodity but such as was absolutely necessary, to trade with no importer or person buying his goods of importers, and holding him who should break this agreement as dishonored and an enemy to the liberties of his country.

As illustrating the loyalty of the people to the King and Parliament. A glance at the report of a committee, consisting of William Young, David Bancroft, Samuel Curtis, Timothy Bigelow and Stephen Salisbury, will suffice. This committee was appointed at a town meeting held in March, 1773, to consider the contents of the celebrated Boston Pamphlet; which committee presented an elaborate report at the adjournment in the May following. Appealing to the record of the past as proof of their loyalty, they declare "the fond affection that has ever subsisted in our hearts for Great Britain and its sovereign, has ever induced us to esteem it above any other country; and as fond children speak of a father's house, we have ever called it our home, and always have been ready to rejoice when they rejoiced, to weep when they have wept, and whenever required, to bleed when they have bled; and in return, we are sorry to say, we have had our harbor filled with ships of war, in a hostile manner, and troops posted in our metropolis in a time of profound peace; not only posted in a manner greatly insulting, but actually slaughtering the inhabitants; cannon leveled against our senate house; the fortress or key of the Province taken from us; and as an addition to our distress, the commander-in-chief of the Province has declared he has not the power to control the troops. Nevertheless we are ready and willing to stand forth in defence of the King of Great Britain, his crown and dignity, and our noble constitution, and when called to it, risk our lives; and in that day let him that hath no sword, sell his garment and buy one."

At this meeting a Committee of Correspondence was chosen to correspond with committees in the other towns in this Province, this committee consisting of William Young, Timothy Bigelow and John Smith.

The origin of the scheme for forming Committees of Correspondence is credited by Tudor in his life of James Otis, to the Hon. James Warren of Plymouth. He communicated it to Samuel Adams who was making him a visit. Mr. Adams consulted with his friends on his return to Boston, the plan was adopted, spread with rapidity throughout all the colonies, and became one of the most powerful means for uniting and directing public sentiment in favor of the Revolution.

At the close of the year 1773, a Society was formed, which became a most efficient means toward effecting the purposes of the patriots of the town. This organization had its origin in the necessity for unity of purpose and action, in counteracting royal influence; and although it existed less than three years, it was, during its existence, a powerful medium for carrying out the popular will. The prominent part assumed by this society, in the proceedings of the times, would seem to justify a reproduction of its Rules and Regulations, showing the objects to be attained, the methods of procedure, and a partial insight into the customs of the period.

THE AMERICAN POLITICAL SOCIETY. *

Worcester, New England, Dec. 27, 1773.

At a meeting held at the house of Asa Ward, at 5 o'clock in the afternoon, Joshua Bigelow was chosen chairman.

A motion was made and seconded, that a vote be put whether the meeting shall be continued from time to time, to take under our consideration and debate upon, such matters and things as concern our rights and liberties, and whether the members present would enter into a society covenant for said purpose under good and wholesome rules and regulations.

Carried Unanimously.

A committee was chosen, consisting of Nathan Baldwin, Samuel Curtis and Timothy Bigelow, to report a code of Rules and Regulations, and the meeting adjourned to the 3rd day of January, 1774. At that time the committee presented the following, which was adopted.

RULES AND REGULATIONS.

Whereas, at this present time, the good people of this country in general (and with respect to some particular circumstances the town of

---

* From the original records in possession of the American Antiquarian Society.

Worcester in particular,) labor under many impositions and burdens grevious to be borne, which we apprehend would never have been imposed upon us, if we had been united, and opposed the machinations of some designing persons in this Province, who are grasping at power, and the property of their neighbors; for the prevention whereof, and the bettter securing our liberties and properties, and counteracting the designs of our enemies, we, whose names are hereunto subscribed, do by these presents incorporate ourselves into a society by the name of The American Political Society, and to meet at some public house in Worcester, at least once every month, to advise with each other on proper methods to be pursued by us, and each of us, respecting our common rights and liberties, civil and religious; and for the regular ordering and conducting our said society in their meetings, they shall choose some one of the members of said society as a chairman to preside in said meeting or meetings; to keep up good order, and an observance of the rules hereafter mentioned; and one other member as a clerk, to keep an exact journal of the acts and proceedings of this our society, in their said meetings, and for the well ordering our said society, the following rules shall be strictly observed and complied with by each and every member thereof, viz:

1st. That no discourse or transaction in any of our meetings shall be communicated or divulged to any person or persons not belonging to our said society, by any ways or means whatever, (such only excepted as are allowed to be made public by the unanimous vote of our said society,) and that if any person or persons shall be guilty of a breach of this article, he or they be punished with expulsion from our said society.

2nd. That we will avoid all law suits with all men as much as possible in general, and in particular with any or either of the members of this our society, and if it shall so happen that a difference shall arise between any two or more of the members thereof in any of our meetings, and the parties cannot settle it to their satisfaction between themselves, they shall submit it to the determination of the society thereon or be expelled the society.

3rd. That each member of the society shall, as he hath opportunity, promote the interests of every member of this society, in all honest ways and methods that he can, without hurting his own or the interests of any other member of this society.

4th. That in our said meetings, if any member knows of any infringements of the common rights of mankind, he shall make the same known.

5th. That whenever any member hath anything to offer in a speech to the society assembled, he shall address himself to the chairman then presiding, and during the time of his speaking he shall not be broken in upon or interrupted by any person whatever but by leave of the chairman.

6th. That in all and every of our monthly meetings, our expenses for liquor, &c., shall not exceed six pence per man upon an average, and in our quarterly meetings, it shall not exceed two shillings per man as aforesaid upon an average.

7th. That each member of the society is debarred the liberty of asking, inviting or introducing any person whatever into our company, without first having obtained leave of our society for so doing.

8th. That each member shall constantly attend all our said meetings, and if any member shall fail of attending, he shall forfeit and pay into the hands of the clerk, six pence for the use of the society, for such his non-attendance, and at that rate for every such offence, except he can assign reasons for his non-attendance satisfactory to the society.

9th. That every member of our said society shall have full power to dismiss himself from said society in the following manner, viz: by informing them in any one of their meetings, in writing, that he will inviolably keep all the secrets of said society, as faithfully as if he still belonged to it himself and as they desire, but that he desires a dismission by a vote of said society, and that it may be entered on the journal of the transactions of said society, that he was dismissed by his own desire.

10th. That each particular member of this our said society, reposing special trust and confidence in every other member of the society, looks upon himself as bound, and hereby binds himself by the ties of honor, virtue, truth, sincerity, and every appellation that is dear to him in this life, faithfully and truly to keep and perform for himself, each and every of the articles herein mentioned and expressed, to all intents and purposes.

At an adjourned meeting Jan. 10, the following were added.

11th. That there shall be a new choice of officers in said society, at each meeting next following a quarterly meeting.

12th. That no member be admitted into this society but by a majority of the votes, and that the vote be by ballot.

13th. That each of our said meetings begin at five of the clock P. M., and not to continue over four hours, quarterly meetings excepted.

14th. That our monthly meetings shall be on the first Monday of February, second Monday of March, first Monday of May, June, August, September, November and December.

And that our quarterly meetings shall be on the first Monday of April, July, October and January, and all quarterly meetings to begin at two of the clock P. M.

The original membership consisted of thirty-one individuals; others joining from time to time, made a total membership of seventy-one.

ORIGINAL MEMBERS.

Joshua Bigelow,	Samuel Woodburn,	Ebenezer Lovell,
Benjamin Flagg,	Josiah Pierce,	Joseph Barber,
Thomas Wheeler,	Samuel Curtis,	Samuel McCracken,
William Young,	Jonas Hubbard,	David Chadwick,
Timothy Bigelow,	Joshua Whitney,	James Barber,
John Smith,	John Kelso,	William Dana,
Robert Smith,	Ebenezer Holbrook, Jr.	Thomas Lyndes,
Jacob Hemenway,	Amos Wheeler,	Samuel Fullerton,
Francis Harrington,	Nathan Baldwin,	William Johnson,
David Thomas,	John Pierce,	John Emerson.
	Edward Crafts,	

JOINED SUBSEQUENTLY.

Silas Moore,	Joseph Ball,	Jonathan Lovell,
Cyprian Stevens,	William Treadwell,	Ebenezer Willington,
Jona. Gleason,	Ezekiel Howe,	Robert Gray,
Samuel Whitney,	Jonathan Rice,	Samuel Brown,
Thaddeus Bigelow,	Daniel Beard,	Oliver Pierce,
John Woodward,	Ephraim Miller,	Dr. John Green,
Benjamin Chapin,	Moses Miller,	Elijah Harrington,
Jno. Barnard,	Reuben Gray,	Robert Crawford,
Daniel Harris,	Asa Ward,	Benjamin Flagg, Jr.,
Phinehas Jones,	James Moore,	William Taylor,
Jacob Holmes,	Jonathan Stone,	Samuel Miller,
Ebenezer Wiswall,	Thomas Knight,	David Bancroft,
Wm. Jennison Sterne,	Levi Houghton,	Phinehas Ward,
	Josiah Knight.	

Feb. 7, 1774. A debate was had upon the impropriety of choosing any person to any office, who was not an open and professed friend to constitutional liberty.

Feb. 25. They agreed upon a plan of procedure for the March meeting.

April 4. It was voted "that the Committee of Correspondence be directed to notify the committees in the several towns in the county, that the vote for County Treasurer had not been counted at the late Court of General Sessions of the Peace, as had been customary, and warned them of the dangers consequent thereupon, that the people might be on their guard against fraud and deception." And also voted that " this society will each one bear and pay their equal part of the fine and charges that may be laid upon Messrs. Joshua Bigelow and Timothy Bigelow, for their refusal to be empanneled upon the Grand Jury, at our next Superior Court of Assize, for the County of Worcester, if they shall be chosen into that office; and their refusal is founded upon the principle that they cannot consistently with good conscience and order, serve, if Peter Oliver, Esq., is present on the bench as Chief Justice, or Judge of said Court, before he is lawfully tried and acquitted from the high crimes and charges for which he now stands impeached by the Honorable House of Representatives, and the major part of the Grand Jurors for the whole county join them in refusing to serve for the reasons aforesaid."

A committee was chosen to prepare instructions for the Representative that should be chosen to serve the town in that office, at the annual meeting in May.

May 2d. It was debated whether the Rev. Mr. Maccarty's additional salary of the sum of £20 be taken off for the year. John Kelso was chosen Grand Juror for the year. June 10. It was voted unanimously, " for the better securing our injured rights and privileges," to sign a Solemn League and Covenant, not to purchase any English goods, until the port and harbor of Boston shall be opened. July 4th. Voted that each member of the society be provided with powder, flint and lead. Aug. 1st. Nathan Baldwin, Joshua Bigelow, Benjamin Flagg, Dr. John Green, Ebenezer Lovell, Timothy Bigelow and Lieut. Samuel Curtis, were chosen a committee to prepare a plan of action to be pursued at the town meeting, to be held Aug. 22d. Aug. 18. "Voted that Nathan Perry be moderator of our next town meeting, if he shall be chosen to that office; if not, then Josiah Pierce shall preside." Oct. 3d. The instructions to Joshua Bigelow and Timothy Bigelow, to be adopted at town meeting Oct. 4, were considered and approved. Nov. 7. David Bancroft and Jonathan Stone were chosen a committee to wait upon and present the Solemn League and Covenant to the following persons: Rev. Thaddeus Maccarty, Col. Gardner Chandler, Dr. Elijah Dix, Stephen Salisbury and Timothy Paine, Esq. Dec. 5th. Joshua Bigelow was instructed to lay before the County Congress, the refusal of Gardner Chandler to sign the Solemn League and Covenant. Sept. 5, 1775, a committee consisting of Samuel McCracken, Josiah Peirce, David Bigelow, Samuel Woodburn and Nathan Baldwin, was chosen to inspect the tories going and coming from Lancaster or any other way. In 1776, divisions having sprung up on some points, among which was the propriety of the society controlling the town meetings, and assuming powers properly belonging to the Committee of Correspondence, an attempt was made to harmonize conflicting opinions, and a committee of inquiry was chosen to investigate the matter and endeavor to effect a compromise. After several meetings, and affairs remaining unimproved, and also in view of the fact that a large proportion of the members were absent in the army, it was voted, May 20, 1776, " that we separate at the next meeting," which was probably done, as there is no record of the June meeting.

While a majority of the people of this town were aware that the acts of the British Ministry were tending to deprive them of all participation in the affairs of government, and to reduce them to a condition of dependance and servility, there was a formidable party composed in great part of the leading citizens of the town, persons in high standing who had held high civil and military offices, and enjoyed the confidence and esteem of all the people, who considered all acts designed to resist the encroachments of the English Government as treasonable and rebellious, and who cast the whole weight of their wealth, talents and influence on the side of royal prerogative.

The patriots of Worcester found these " internal enemies" or tories, one of the greatest obstacles to overcome ; the royal influence being far more powerful in the interior of the Province, than in the eastern counties.

In a warrant issued for a town meeting to be held at the meeting house March 7th, 1774, an article was inserted calling upon the town " to consider, and act, and vote as they may think proper," upon a request of twenty-seven of the free holders and other inhabitants of said town, relating to an act of Parliament giving a privilege to the East India Company to export teas to America, subject to duty, to raise a revenue for his Majesty. At this meeting, a committee consisting of William Young, Josiah Pierce and Timothy Bigelow, was chosen to take the article into consideration, and report in two hours. At the expiration of that time they presented a report, which was accepted. After particularizing some of the most intolerable grievances from which they were suffering, they came to the consideration of the main subject named in the article, the exportation of teas to America, subject to duty. The committee submitted a resolution, which was accordingly adopted, refusing to buy, sell, or in any way to be concerned with India teas of any kind, until the act imposing such a duty be repealed; and also resolving, to break off all commercial intercourse with those persons, in this or any other place, who should act counter to these resolutions; and further resolving that "we have an indisputable right, at this time, and at all times, boldly to assert our rights and make known our grievances, being sensible that the freedom of speech and security of property always go together. None but the base tyrant and his wicked tools dread this liberty; upright measures will defend themselves. It is not only our indubitable right but a requisite duty, in this legal and public manner to make known our grievances. Among the many benefits that will naturally result therefrom will be, we hope, that important one of undeceiving our gracious sovereign, who from the wicked measures practised against us we have just reason to suppose has been artfully deluded; in defence of whose sacred person, crown and dignity, together with our natural and constitutional rights, we are ready at all times boldly to risk our lives and fortunes."

Accompanying this report on the record, is the following protest signed by some of the leading royalists of the town.

We whose names are underwritten, beg leave to enter our dissent and protest against the vote of the town of Worcester, relating to the fourth article in the warrant for the town meeting March, 1774, and do accordingly sign this as protest against the acceptance of the report of the committee thereon.

March 7, 1774.

James Putnam,
John Chandler,
Daniel Ward,
John Curtis,
Daniel Boyden,
William Campbell,
Nathaniel Moore,
Rufus Chandler,
John Mower,

William Paine,
Nahum Willard,
David Moore,
James Hart, Jr.
Samuel Moore,
Cornelius Stowell,
Andrew Duncan,
Palmer Goulding,
Samuel Mower,

James Goodwin,
Samuel Bridge,
David Bancroft,
Jacob Stevens,
Jonas Nichols,
Gershom Rice, Jr.
Darius Boyden,
Joseph Blair.

Although the protest was entered on the record, it was rejected by the town.

At a town meeting held May 16, Mr. Joshua Bigelow was chosen Representative, and a committee consisting of Messrs. Josiah Pierce, Samuel Curtis, Stephen Salisbury, Timothy Bigelow, John Kelso, Joshua Whitney and Edward Crafts, was appointed to draw up instructions for his observance. At an adjourned meeting held May 20th, this committee reported the following which was adopted.

Mr. Joshua Bigelow,

Sir: As English America is in a general alarm, in consequence of some late unconstitutional stretches of power, we are sensible this is the most difficult period that hath ever yet commenced since the arrival of our ancestors into this unexplored, uncultivated wilderness; and being fully sensible that the wisest head, uprightest heart, and firmest resolution, are the necessary qualifications of the person fit and suitable to represent us in the Great and General Court of this Province, the present year, we have honored you with our suffrages for that important office. Notwithstanding our confidence in your virtue and abilities, we think it necessary to prescribe some certain rules for your conduct.

And first, as there is a late act of the British Parliament, to be enforced in America, with troops and ships of war, on the first day of June, in order to stop the port and harbor of Boston, thereby depriving us of the winds and seas, which God and Nature gave in common to mankind, we are induced to believe that the Ministers of Great Britain, through misinformation, are led to a prostitution of that power which has heretofore made Europe tremble, to abridge us, their brethren in this Province, of our natural and civil rights, notwithstanding. Exclusive of our natural rights, we had all the privileges and immunities of Englishmen confirmed to us by our royal charter. And as we view this hostile maneuver of Great Britain as a blow aimed, through Boston, at the whole of American liberties, being emboldened through a consciousness of the justice of our cause, we, in the most solemn manner, direct you, that whatever measures Great Britain may take to distress us, you be not in the least intimidated, and thereby induced, that whatever requisitions, or ministerial mandate there may be, in order to subject us to any unconstitutional acts of the British Parliament, to comply therewith. But to the utmost of your power, resist the most distant approaches to slavery. But more particularly, should the people of this Province, through their representatives, be required to compensate the East India Company for the loss of their tea, we hereby lay the strictest injunction on you not to comply therewith. As the destruction of the tea was not a public act, we cannot see the justice of a public demand. As the civil law is open to punish the offenders, we rather think instead of an equitable compensation, it would be the means of encouraging riots and robberies, and of consequence, render the courts of justice of no use.

We also earnestly require that a strict union of the colonists be one of the first objects in your view, and that you carefully and immediately pursue every legal measure that may tend thereto, viz: that Committees of Correspondence be kept up between the several Houses of Assembly through the colonies; and that you by no means fail to use your utmost endeavor, that there by a general Congress formed of deputies from the same; that so we may unite in some safe and sure plan, to secure and defend the American liberties at this important crisis of affairs.

Also, we direct you, as soon as may be, to endeavor that Peter Oliver, Esq., be brought to answer to the impeachment against him, preferred by the Representatives of this Province in the name of the whole people.

There are a number of other matters respecting the internal policy of this Province, that in our opinion, at this season, require the attention of the legislator; but, at a time like this, when Britain in return for the blood we have, on every needful occasion, so freely shed in her cause, has reduced thousands, through a wanton exercise of power, in our metropolis, to the most distressing circumstances, which, at first view, is sufficient to excite in the human breast every tender and compasionate feeling. This is enough to engross your whole attention. Should other matters come under your consideration, in the course of the present year, relative to the common and ordinary exigencies of government, we make not the least doubt, you will on your part, make the peace and prosperity of the whole Province your ultimate aim and end, and by that means honor yourself and us, your constituents, in the choice we have made."

Strong efforts were made on the part of the royalists to prevent the acceptance of the report of the committee. Col. Putnam, than whom there were few, if any, abler lawyers in North America, threw the whole weight of his influence, learning and ability against its adoption, his efforts being seconded by many of the ablest and most influential men in town. On the question of the acceptance and adoption of the report the adherents of the King were defeated. In the hope of obtaining a reconsideration of the votes, a petition signed by 43 freeholders was presented to the selectmen, requesting them to call a town meeting for that purpose, and in accordance with this request, the following warrant was issued.

WARRANT.

WORCESTER, SS.

To Samuel Bridge, one of the Constables of the Town of Worcester, GREETING.

Whereas a great number of the freeholders, inhabitants and voters in said town of Worcester, preferred a petition to us, the subscribers, Selectmen of said Town, setting forth that there have been of late divers commotions and disturbances in many towns and places within the Province, and many actions of a riotous nature and dangerous tendency have been done and committed, whereby the property of many of his Majesty's good and peaceable subjects has been destroyed, their persons insulted, and their lives endangered, more especially in the town of Boston, and that by the artful practices of some people there, under the pretence of Patriotism, but with evil intentions and making unrighteous gain to themselves by the ruin and destruction of others, a spirit of opposition to all law, order and good government has been raised and propagated in many towns and places within this Province, and some having been so far seduced that they have unwarrantably adopted measures subversive of public liberty and the good order of the State, and destructive of the peace of society, and in some places votes and resolves have been passed which they have seen published, approving or justifying the unwarrantable and riotous proceedings of the said town of Boston, and have thereby, as they fear, in some measures made themselves partakers of their guilt, and wishing to avoid the reproach and imputations of any such guiltiness falling on them, they desire to bear their public testimony against all riots, unlawful assemblies, acts of violence, oppression and robbery, more especially would they manifest their utter detestation and abhorence of that unparalleled act of violence, the destruction of the teas, the last winter in Boston, and also against the unlawful force and violence in divers riotous acts committed on the persons and properties of sundry good people in this Province, to whom said teas were consigned, and at the annual meeting in Worcester, in March last, certain resolves were passed and voted to be entered on the records of the town of Worcester, against the express will and opinion of the respectable inhabitants of the town then assembled, and had not the members of the committee who made or copied the resolves, voted for their being accepted and recorded, there would have been a majority of the town against the acceptance of them, and at that time many of the sober, judicious people of this town thought that those resolves were calculated to serve seditious purposes, and some of them did therefore enter their protest in writing against the said resolves and proceedings, and desired the same might be entered and recorded with the records of the town, yet hoping to prevent it, the town did unreasonably and hastily vote that the said protestation should not be received or recorded, and they have reason to apprehend there are many more persons of consideration and interest within said town that did not then protest for want of opportunity to do it, that would be glad of a fit time for doing it, and discovering their mind on many late acts and proceedings, in a public manner, and they are of opinion that were the same matters now again to be considered and acted on by the town, their proceedings would be very different from what they were before, at least that such a number would now protest, and would before had they been present as are owners and proprietors of by far the largest share of the interest and property of the whole town, and praying that a meeting of the said town may be warned that the inhabitants being voters may be assembled, as soon as may be, and so have an opportunity of declaring their sentiments, and acting with freedom in a legal way, with respect to the votes, resolves, protestations and so forth, before referred to, and to examine into the proceedings and conduct of certain persons in the town of Worcester, styling themselves the Committee of Correspondence for the town, and that their power and authority may be examined into, and they required to lay before the town, all their proceedings and doings as a committee, together or apart, since they have assumed that character, and that they lay before the town, all such advices, letters and intelligence as they or any of them shall have received, and from whom they had it relating to public matters, and produce true copies of all such advices and letters as they or any of them in the course of their correspondence have communicated to others, that the town may have a full and fair opportunity of publicly examining into their whole conduct and proceedings, as by said petition appears.

You are therefore hereby required in his Majesty's name, in the usual way and manner, to warn and give notice to the freeholders and other inhabitants of the said town qualified according to law to vote in town affairs, to meet and assemble at the meeting house in said town, on Monday the twentieth day of June next, at three o'clock in the afternoon, then and there to choose

1st. A Moderator.

2d. To act on the several matters and things contained in said pepetition, and to receive the report of the Committee of Correspondence in relation to their proceedings, as therein mentioned, and for the town to act on all matters mentioned in said petition, as they may judge proper.

Hereof fail not, and make return of this warrant with your doings to some of the Selectmen before said meeting.

Dated at Worcester, the thirtieth day of May, in the Fourteenth year of his Majesty's Reign, Anno Domini, 1774,

TIMOTHY PAINE,
WILLIAM YOUNG,
THOMAS WHEELER,
JOSIAH PIERCE,
} Selectmen.

In accordance with this warrant a meeting was held at the designated time and place, and after a long and stormy debate, the patriotic party prevailed. The tories still unwilling to yield, offered a protest, which was refused. The Town Clerk, Mr. Clark Chandler, a firm and persistent royalist, entered a copy of this protest on the records of the town. Copies were also inserted in the Boston News Letter, of June 30, and the Massachusetts Gazette of July 4, 1774, being prefaced with the following note.

MESSRS. PRINTERS:

If you please you may give the following protestation of us a few friends of truth, peace and order, a place in your paper; for it is believed that we and many others through the Province, have too long already held our peace.

"At a meeting of the inhabitants of the town of Worcester, held there on the 20th day of June, A. D., 1774, pursuant to an application made to the Selectmen by 43 voters and freeholders of the same town, dated the 20th day of May last, therein among other things, declaring their just apprehensions of the fatal consequences that may follow the many riotous and seditious actions that have of late times been done and perpetrated in divers places within this Province; the votes and proceedings of which meeting are by us deemed irregular and arbitrary: Wherefore we, some of us who were petitioners for the said meeting, and others, inhabitants of the town, hereunto subscribing, thinking it our indispensable duty, in these times of discord and confusion in too many of the towns within this Province, to bear testimony in the most open and unreserved manner against all riotous, disorderly and seditious practices, must therefore now declare, that it is with the deepest concern for public peace and order, that we behold so many, whom we used to esteem sober, peaceable men, so far deceived, deluded and led astray, by the artful, crafty and insidious practices of some evil-minded and ill-disposed persons, who, under the disguise of patriotism, and falsely styling themselves the friends of liberty, some of them neglecting their own proper business and occupation, in which they ought to be employed for the support of their families, spending their time in discoursing of matters they do not understand, raising and propagating falsehoods and calumnies of those men they look up to with envy, and on whose fall and ruin they wish to rise, intend to reduce all things to a state of tumult, discord and confusion.

And in pursuance of those evil purposes and practices, they have imposed on the understanding of some, corrupted the principles of others, and distracted the minds of many, who under the influence of this delusion, have been tempted to act a part that may prove, and that has already proved, extremely prejudicial to the Province, and as it may be, fatal to themselves; bringing into real danger, and in many instances destroying, that liberty and property we all hold sacred, and which they vainly and impiously boast of defending at the expense of their blood and treasure.

And, as it appears to us, that many of this town seem to be led aside by strange opinions, and are prevented coming to such prudent votes and resolutions as might be for the general good and advantage of this town in particular, agreeably to the request of the petitioners for this meeting,—

And as the town has refused to dismiss the persons styling themselves the Committee of Correspondence for the town, and has also refused so much as to call on them to render an account of their past dark and pernicious proceedings,—

We therefore, whose names are hereunto subscribed, do each of us declare and protest, it is our firm opinion, that the Committees of Correspondence in the several towns in this Province, being creatures of modern invention, and constituted as they be, are a legal grievance, having no legal foundation, contrived by a junto to serve particular designs and purposes of their own, and that they, as they have been and are now managed in this town, are a nuisance. And we fear, it is in a great measure owing to the baneful influence of such committees, that the teas of immense value, lately belonging to the East India Company, were, not long since, scandalously destroyed in Boston, and that many other enormous acts of violence and oppression have been perpetrated, whereby the lives of many honest worthy persons, have been endangered and their property destroyed.

It is by these committees also, that papers have been lately published, and are now circulating through the Province, inviting and wickedly tempting, all persons to join them, fully implying, if not expressly denouncing the destruction of all that refuse to subscribe those unlawful combinations, tending directly to sedition, civil war, and rebellion.

These and all such enormities, we detest and abhor, and the authors of them we esteem enemies of our King and country, violators of all law and civil liberty, the malevolent disturbers of the peace of society, subverters of the established constitution, and enemies of mankind:

William Elder,	Nathan Patch,	Daniel Moore,
Daniel Ward,	Samuel Mower, Jr,	James Hart, Jr.
John Walker,	Isaac Moore,	Cornelius Stowell,
Nathaniel Adams,	Joshua Johnson,	Israel Stevens,
William Campbell,	John Chandler,	Jonathan Phillips,
Samuel Moore,	Gardner Chandler,	Samuel Brooks,
John Mower,	James Putnam,	Isaac Willard,
Joseph Blair,	Daniel Boyden,	Jacob Stevens,
Micah Johnson,	John Curtis,	Joseph Clark,
Edmund Heard,	Thomas Baird,	Isaac Barnard,
Thomas Baird, Jr.	James Hart,	William Paine,
Samuel Mower,	Elisha Smith,	Thaddeus Chamberlain,
Samuel Bridge,	Tyrus Rice,	John Chamberlain,
Jacob Chamberlin,	Nahum Willard,	William Curtis,
Andrew Duncan,	Rufus Chandler,	Abel Stowell,
James Goodwin,	Palmer Goulding,	Daniel Goulding,
Clark Chandler,	Adam Walker,	William Chandler.
Israel Jennison,		

The patriots were not aware for some time, that this protest was entered on the records of the town, and when this fact was discovered, a storm of indignation was aroused, so violent that many of the royalists were alarmed for their personal safety. A petition signed by Joshua Bigelow and fourteen others, was presented to the Selectmen, characterizing the protest as a false and scandalous attack on the inhabitants, the committee and their doings, charging the Town Clerk with violating his trust, and requesting them to issue their warrant for a meeting to take the subject into consideration. A meeting was called August 22d, at which Nathan Perry was chosen moderator, and it was voted that Joshua Bigelow, Jonas Hubbard, David Bancroft, Samuel Curtis, Jonathan Stone, Benjamin Flagg and Josiah Pierce be a committee to take under their consideration the protest of William

Elder, John Curtis and others, and make report to the town of their doings thereon, at the adjournment of the meeting. At the adjourned meeting held on the 24th, the committee reported the following resolutions, which were adopted :

"Whereas, the publication in the Massachusetts Gazette of June 30th, was made as a protest of the signers of it against the proceedings of the town of Worcester, and contains in it a number of groundless reflections and aspersions against the inhabitants of the town, for it seems to be implied in the direction to the printer, published at the front of the protest, that the signers were the only persons in the town who were friends to truth, peace and order, and that they were the only persons, that had any just apprehensions of the ill consequences arising by mobs, riots, &c., and that all the rest of the inhabitants acted irregularly and arbitrarily, notwithstanding the matters voted in said meeting were fairly considered; and that they were so destitute of understanding as to be led astray, by evil minded persons, who were endeavoring to reduce all things to a state of disorder and confusion, thereby making themselves the sole judges of what is rule and order, and what is not; and proceed to stigmatize the inhabitants as holding to such bad opinions, as to prevent the town's acting prudently and for the general good. It is also implied in the publication, that this town allows a number of persons in it, to assume the character of a Committee of Correspondence for the town, and to act darkly and perniciously with impunity, contrary to rule and good order, and in violation of the truth, after, with unparalleled arrogance, representing themselves as the only friends to it, they assert that the town has refused to dismiss the persons styling themselves a Committee of Correspondence for the town, when, setting aside the inconsistency of the towns dismissing persons who had arrogated the character of a committee, and consequently were in fact not chosen by the town, they well knew that the town had not been requested, either to dismiss persons styling themselves a committee, or those gentlemen so denominated by the town; neither was there any article in the warrant for calling said meeting, to dismiss any persons whatever from office, nor so much as proposed in the meeting. There is also a malignity cast upon Committees of Correspondence in general through the continent, and in particular against the committee chosen by this town, without any reason assigned for the same, but the opinion of the protesters, too slender a foundation to asperse the character of town officers upon, and they have endeavored to insinuate into the minds of the public, that the men of which Committees of Correspondence are composed through the Province, are a parcel of unprincipled knaves, who are endeavoring to destroy the lives and property of the peaceful and well disposed, and also alleging that it is by these committees that papers have been lately published, and that they have wickedly tempted all persons to sign them, which they call an unlawful combination, tending directly to civil war and rebellion. This town knows of no such paper; if it be the non-consumption agreement, entered and entering into, through this and neighboring Provinces, that is pointed at, we take it upon us to say, that we much approve of the same, that if strictly adhered to it will save our money, promote industry, frugality, and our own manufacturers, and tend directly to prevent civil war and rebellion.

" After offering their opinions of mobs, riots, tumults and disorder, and the proceedings of the town, so cruelly and with such temerity, as shows them to be destitute of that humanity and christian charity which we in all duty owe one to the other, that brand all who do not join with them, with the characters of enemies of the King and country, violators of all law and civil liberty, the malevolent disturbers of society, subverters of the established constitution, and enemies of mankind. And as it appears by the said publication, that the same is recorded in the town book, notwithstanding the many aspersions it contained against the people of this town, and without the liberty or knowledge of the town. Therefore,

" Voted, that the town clerk do, in the presence of the town, obliterate, erase, or otherwise deface the said recorded protest, and the names thereto subscribed, so that it may become utterly illegible and unintelligible.

" Voted, that the method taken by the leaders, in protesting, and procuring a very considerable number to sign the protest who are not voters in the town, we think was a piece of low cunning, to deceive the public, and make their party appear more numerous and formidable than it was in reality.

" Voted, that the signers of said protest, on some of whom the town has conferred many favors, and consequently might expect their kindest and best services, be deemed unworthy of holding any town office or honor, until they have made satisfaction for their offence to the acceptance of the town, which ought to be made as public as the protest was.

"Voted, that as it is highly needful that those of the signers who have not made satisfaction as aforesaid, should be known in future, it is therefore necessary that their names be inserted as follows, viz:

  James Putnam,   William Paine,
  Isaac Moore,   John Walker,
     Joshua Johnson.

"Voted, that the following admonition be given to the town clerk.

"*Mr. Clark Chandler:* Whereas this town, at their annual meeting in March last, as well as for several years before, honored you by choosing you for their clerk, relying on your fidelity, that you would act for the honor of the town, and find themselves much disappointed, by your conduct in recording on the town book the scandalous protest of William Elder and others, filled with falsehood and reflections against the town, we have just reason to fear you were actuated in the matter by unjustifiable motives, and, at this time, exhort you to be more circumspect in the execution of the duties of your office, and never give this town the like trouble of calling a town meeting again on such an occasion. The town wish to see your behavior such as may restore you to their former good opinion of you.

"Whereas the Committee of Correspondence for this town willingly laid all their proceedings before the town, when requested, and it thereby appears, notwithstanding the ungenerous abuse heaped on them by the protesters, that they have acted with care, diligence and caution, therefore, voted, that the thanks of this town be given to the committee for their circumspection, and that they be directed to go on, with their former vigilance, in corresponding with the other committees of the several towns in this Province."

In accordance with the vote, the clerk was required to expunge the recorded protest from the town book, which he did by scrolling with a pen, but the temper of the meeting was such that it would not allow a word to remain legible, and he was required to dip his fingers in the ink and draw them over the first page of the protest several times. These pages are an interesting memento of the times, and speak in tones not to be mistaken, of the stern determination which possessed the patriotic party of the town. They are contained in Vol. 4 of the town records, in custody of the City Clerk.

At this meeting, it was voted that the selectmen be a committee to receive any article of provisions which the inhabitants should contribute for the relief of the poor of the town of Boston, and also voted that Daniel Beard, Dr. John Green, John Smith, David Bigelow, and Samuel Miller, be a committee to take under their consideration the acts of the British Parliament respecting America, and report to the town of their doings at the adjournment of the meeting; and also voted, that Jonathan Stone, David Bancroft, Josiah Pierce, Jonathan Rice, and David Chadwick be a committee to offer those persons who had not signed the agreement or covenant for the non-consumption of British goods, an opportunity to do the same.

On the evening previous to the meeting of the 22d, the protesters, having been notified by the Committee of Correspondence that satisfaction would be demanded from them by the town, met at the King's Arms Tavern,* and signed a recantation of the protest. This document afterwards appeared in the Massachusetts Gazette and Boston News Letter of Sept. 15th, and the Boston Evening Post of Sept. 19th, 1774, and was prefaced by the note below. Whether the reasons given in the preface were those which prompted their recantation, or whether the indignation of the people caused them to seek refuge from the storm that they had aroused, is a question perhaps as yet unsolved.

"TO THE PRINTERS: The following recantation, signed by forty-three of the Worcester Protesters, in part serves to show how the now more conspicuously corrupt measures of the British Ministry in the

---

*On the site occupied at present by the Lincoln House.

Canada Papist Act, etc., unites all parties. Those among us that have heretofore seemed to favor the side of Prerogative, have, since their conduct became so barefaced, joined themselves to the people; all indiscriminately flying to arms, and marching to the defence of our country when we had intelligence that our brethren were again butchered by a merciless soldiery, is a sufficient proof that we are one and all determined not to survive our liberties, however we might before differ in some unessentials.

WORCESTER, Sept. 5, 1774.

"Whereas, we the subscribers, have given the good people of this Province in general, and the inhabitants of the town of Worcester in particular, just cause to be offended with each of us in that unguarded action of ours in signing and protesting in the Massachusetts Gazette of June 30th, a certain piece of our protest against the vote and proceedings of the town of Worcester, on the 20th of June, 1774, wherein we acknowledge we have cast cruel aspersions upon the town of Worcester and upon the Committee of Correspondence for said town, and upon all Committees of Correspondence throughout the Province, for which we are sorry, and take this opportunity publicly to manifest it, and declare we did not so well consider the contents, and that we had no other intention than to bear our testimony against mobs and riots, notwithstanding anything in said protest to the contrary; and that we have that charity to our fellow townsmen, as to believe that they will heartily join with us in this particular, for to the best of our knowledge we declare that the present generation in this town has never been concerned in any mobs or riots in this or any other place. And we hereby beg their forgiveness, and all others we may have offended; also that we may be restored to their favor, and be made partakers of that inestimable blessing, the good will of our neighbors and the whole community.

William Elder,	Gardner Chandler,	Isaac Willard,
Nathaniel Adams,	Daniel Boyden,	Jacob Stevens,
Samuel Moore,	John Curtis,	Joseph Clark,
John Mower,	Thomas Baird,	Isaac Barnard,
Joseph Blair,	James Hart,	John Chamberlain,
Micah Johnson,	Elisha Smith,	William Curtis,
Edmund Heard,	Tyrus Rice,	Abel Stowell,
Thomas Baird, Jr.	Nahum Willard,	Daniel Goulding,
Samuel Mower,	Rufus Chandler,	William Chandler,
Samuel Bridge,	Adam Walker,	John Chandler,

Andrew Duncan,	Daniel Moore,	Jacob Chamberlain,
Clark Chandler,	James Hart, Jr.	Palmer Goulding,
Israel Jennison,	Cornelius Stowell,	James Goodwin,
Nathan Patch,	Jonathan Phillips,	Samuel Brooks,
Samuel Mower, Jr.		

Of the 52 Protesters, 43 signed the above recantation at the King's Arms Tavern; 5 are mentioned in the town vote of Aug. 24, as refusing to give satisfaction, leaving 4 unaccounted for, viz: William Campbell, Daniel Ward, Israel Stevens and Thaddeus Chamberlain. Campbell afterwards publicly recanted. Possibly the other three gave satisfaction in open meeting, or possibly they were not voters, as implied in the resolutions.

CHAPTER III.

The Port Bill—The Mandamus Councillors—Preparation for armed resistance—Court suspended—Recantation of Mr. Campbell—Instruction to Representative to General Court and Delegate to Provincial Congress—Action of the Committee of Safety concerning supplies, Arms, Ammunition, &c.—Drilling of the Minute Men—Call " to arms!" " to arms!" April 19, 1775—March to Boston—Press of Isaiah Thomas removed to Worcester—Letter of John Hancock to Committee of Safety—Tories severely looked after—Worcester men at Bunker Hill—Instruction to Delegate to Provincial Congress—Dr. Willard's recantation.

The rapid succession of oppressive measures enacted by the British Parliament and Ministry, served more and more to inflame the public mind; among these, the Port Bill, that prohibiting the holding of town meetings, and the placing the government of the Province in the hands of the dependents of the King and independent of the people, were especially adapted to increase the irritation.

Among the Councillors appointed by *mandamus* from the King, was the Hon. Timothy Paine of Worcester, a man of marked intellect, high culture, good judgment, sterling integrity and upright life, possessing the highest esteem of his fellow townsmen, who had viewed with alarm the proceedings of the town and people, which he considered rebellious and treasonable. Notwithstanding the high position he had held in the community, it was determined that he should not sit as Councillor. Accordingly on the 22d of August, the people of the neighboring towns were summoned by the Committee of Correspondence to meet with the people of Worcester for the purpose of demanding of him a resignation of his office. " On that day the people to the number of about fifteen hundred * assembled on the common and made choice of five of their number as a committee, viz: Messrs. Joseph Gilbert, John Goulding, Edward Rawson, Thomas Denney, and Joshua Bigelow, to wait on the Hon. Timothy Paine lately appointed Councillor by *mandamus* from his Majesty, to demand of him satisfaction to the people for having qualified himself for said office; and having waited upon him accordingly, he asked them what satisfaction they wanted. They answered a total resignation of his office, and desired him to write it, upon which he withdrew, and in a few minutes, returned with what he had written, which was a total resignation of his office, and a promise never to sit again as Councillor unless agreeably to the charter. He then asked if that was satisfactory. They replied that he must wait on the people, which he thought unreasonable after he had complied with their demands; but they said it was in vain, unless he made his personal appearance the people would not be satisfied, and after their promising to protect him from insult, he waited on them to the body of the people, when Mr. Denney read the resignation, with which numbers were dissatisfied, requiring that Mr. Paine should read it himself, and that with his hat off; he then told the committee that he had complied with all they desired on their promising protection, and that he called upon them for it; but they gave him to understand that the people would not be satisfied till he complied with their demand, which he did, and was then conducted near to his own house by the committee and dismissed. The peo-

---

* This account differs essentially from that given by Lincoln in his History of Worcester. The above is from Gaines' New York Gazetteer and Weekly Mercury of Sept. 5, 1774, and also Rivington's New York Gazetteer of Sept. 8, 1774. It was probably written by some tory, possibly by Mr. Paine himself, and is undoubtedly correct.

ple then drew off, those of each town forming a company, and marching to Rutland, the town in which the Hon. John Murray, another Councillor resided," where after being re-inforced by nearly a thousand men from the Western part of the county, they by a committee called at the house of that gentleman, but not finding him at home left a letter demanding his resignation, with a threat that unless this demand was complied with by the 10th of September they would call on him again.

The decided measures adopted by the patriots alarmed some of the tories, who retired with arms, ammunition and provisions to Stone House hill in Holden, where they remained two or three weeks, after which they returned to their homes.

The aggressive acts of the British authorities in Boston, admonished the people that they must immediately prepare themselves for armed resistance. A company of minute men were enrolled under the command of Capt. Timothy Bigelow, and were daily instructed in the manual of arms, and muskets were procured for their use. The town ordered four cannon to be procured and mounted. An artillery train was organized, of which Edward Crafts was Captain.

Below is an extract of a letter dated Worcester, Sept. 27, 1774.

"Yesterday we had a meeting of all the male inhabitants from the age of 16 to 70, who formed themselves into companies and proceeded to choice of officers—(those who had held commissions under Gov. Hutchinson except a few who resigned them)—one third part of the inhabitants were appointed to be in readiness to march to whatever place their assistance may be wanting. On Friday next, there will be a meeting of the County Committee, in order to remonstrate with Gen. Gage respecting his fortifications at the only entrance by land into our much esteemed capital."

The people being determined that the officers appointed by the Crown should not hold the court sessions, they assembled by invitation of the Committee of Correspondence to the number of several thousand, took possession of the Court House, and compelled the justices to promise in writing never to attempt to exercise their authority contrary to the will of the people. The Court held no sessions for nearly two years, when it was opened under the new government.

At a town meeting held Sept. 26, Joshua Bigelow, David Bancroft, Jonathan Stone and Stephen Salisbury were added to the standing Committee of Correspondence.

A County Convention of Committees of Correspondence was held in Worcester, Sept. 27, and assumed legislative authority, which authority was recognized.

The strength of the royalist party was by this time seriously impaired, a few remained defiant and unsubdued, and concluding that "neither hell, Hull nor Halifax" could afford worse shelter than Worcester gave them, fled to Boston, and placed themselves under the protection of Gen. Gage, and after the evacuation of that town, retired to Halifax. Others sought safety in submission and asked forgiveness in humiliating terms. In the records of the town meeting, held Oct. 17th, occurs the following: "Voted, that the recantation of William Campbell be recorded in the town book and that he be restored to favor."

RECANTATION.

"To the inhabitants of the town of Worcester, Gentlemen: Whereas, I, the subscriber, with a number of others, signed a protest against the proceedings of the town, and the same was published in the Boston Gazette of June last, wherein the inhabitants were unjustly reflected upon in general, and also the whole body of Committees of Correspondence throughout this whole Province, for which I am heartily sorry and ask the forgiveness of all the inhabitants of the town, and the justly offended public; and also for any other offence that I may have given by any means, whether in word or action. I heartily request your acceptance of this sincere acknowledgment; and that if either of the inhabitants hath any other charge against me in regard to my conduct, that he would make it known, that I may have an opportunity of giving christian satisfaction, which I shall ever stand ready to afford. Witness my hand,

WILLIAM CAMPBELL."

At a town meeting held October 4, 1774, Joshua Bigelow was chosen Representative to the General Court, and Timothy Bigelow, Delegate to the Provincial Congress. A committee was chosen to draw up instructions for their government. The committee consisted of David Bancroft, Jonathan Stone, Nathan Baldwin, Samuel Curtis, and Stephen Salisbury; and they reported the following:

"To MR. JOSHUA BIGELOW,

Sir: The Free Electors of the town of Worcester, being greatly alarmed by the unconstitutional authority assumed by the British Parliament in several of their late acts, some of which already have, and others which are intended to operate in this province to the entire subversion of all we hold valuable in our Charter, and which we have indubitable right to enjoy by the laws of Nature and by the principles of the Christian religion, as well as the compact contained in said Charter, therefore that the cruel acts that have been already been put into execution to the great detriment and distress of this Province, and dangerous to the inhabitants of the whole Continent of America, may cease to operate any longer to the entire stoppage of commerce with Great Britain, to the dishonor of his Majesty and the Parliament, and that those other acts which have not yet operated may be prevented from ever being carried into execution, and we thereby reduced to pay obedience to the acts of any future venal, corrupt administration which may deprive us of life and property with impunity, for the prevention whereof, and the security of all and every of our natural and charter rights, we have chosen you to represent us in the Great and General Court of this Province; reposing special trust in your wisdom and fortitude, give you the following instructions as the rule of your conduct respecting the particulars hereafter mentioned, and direct you not to recede from the most rigid virtue in recovering and defending all other of our rights and liberties, not expressly mentioned, that may come under your consideration.

First. Agreeable to the recommendation of the Committee of Correspondence for this county in convention, we instruct you absolutely to refuse to be sworn by any officer or officers but such as are or may be appointed according to the Constitution, or to act as one branch of the legislature in concert with any other, except such as are or may be appointed or supported according to the charter of this Province, and that you refuse to give your attendance at Boston while the town is invested with troops or ships of war; and should there be anything to prevent your acting with such a Governor and Council as is expressly set forth in the charter, that you immediately repair to the town of Concord and there join in a Provincial Congress with such other members as are or may be chosen for that purpose, to extricate this Colony out of its present unhappy circumstances.

Thus far, sir, has the body of this country resolved as the proper instructions for the Representatives that might be chosen in their several towns to meet at Salem; the former part of which, we should have adopted *verbatim* with the addition of several other articles as proper rules for you to have observed as a member of the Great and General Court, provided you have not been excused and discharged therefrom by the Governor's proclamation, the latter we do adopt as proper to direct you to attend at Concord aforesaid, with Mr. Timothy Bigelow, whom we have chosen to represent us in the Provincial Congress to be holden there, and strictly adhere to the instructions given him, for the rule of your conduct in said Congress respecting the particulars therein contained.

By order of the Committee,

DAVID BANCROFT, Chairman."

" To MR. TIMOTHY BIGELOW,

Sir : As you are delegated to represent the inhabitants of the town of Worcester in a Provincial Congress to be convened at Concord, on the second Tuesday of October, instant, the following is offered and enjoined upon you as the instructions of us, your constituents, which you are to observe and follow as a member of said Congress, viz :

As the first Charter given to this Colony was violated and as we think wrongfully wrested from us by Great Britain, and that our second and late Charter is nullified and destroyed by late acts of the British Parliament, by their assuming the authority of making laws binding upon us in all cases whatever, and to enforce our compliance have sent ships of war and blocked the port and harbor of our metropolis, and troops are posted in hostile array to dragoon the people, and the Governor made independent of the people for his support, and mantling our Capital in such a manner as may reduce the worthy inhabitants to a military government: therefore that you endeavor in the most peaceable way and obtain a redress of the following grievances:

First. That the port and harbor of Boston be opened, and the freedom of trade restored, and the King's troops be removed out of this Province, and the command of the fortifications, so called, at the south end of Boston be resigned to the inhabitants, and the commander of the King's troops be prohibited from erecting any fortress or making any intrenchment within the town of Boston or near any of the avenues leading to it.

Second. That the Provincial store of ammunition lately removed by the King's troops from the arsenal at Charlestown be returned to the place from whence it was taken, or into the care of such person or persons as you shall appoint to receive and keep the same for the use of this Province, and that all the ammunition in the magazine in Boston be delivered to the proper owners, if by them requested.

Third. That every one of those incorrigible enemies to this country who have lately been appointed by mandamus from his Majesty as Councillors, and have accepted a seat at the Council Board of this Province, and shall not resign their said office before the second Tuesday of this instant, be impeached as traitors to the Constitution of this Province, and that they be taken into custody and secured for trial.

Fourth. That you endeavor that the Provincial Congress depute an agent or agents from that body, to go to Canada and there treat with its inhabitants in the name and on behalf of the people of this Province, and establish such rules of conduct to be observed by them, as is or may be for the mutual benefit of both, and give assurance to them on our part, of that friendship which some of their inhabitants have nobly displayed in a late generous donation to the oppressed, suffering poor of Boston, for which, we would in this public manner return our grateful thanks; and while we would willingly refund in the same species, if a change of circumstances required it, which, God grant, may never be the case with any of our generous benefactors.

Fifth. That if all the infractions of our rights, by acts of the British Parliament, be not redressed, and we restored to the full enjoyment of all our privileges, contained in the Charter of this Province, granted by their late Majesties, King William and Queen Mary, *to a punctilio,* before the day of your meeting, then, and in that case, you are to consider the people of this Province as absolved, on their part, from the obligation therein contained, and to all intents and purposes reduced to a state of nature; and you are to exert yourself in devising ways and means to raise from the dissolution of the old Constitution, as from the ashes of the Phœnix, a new form, wherein all officers shall be dependent on the suffrages of the people for their existence as such, whatever unfavorable constructions our enemies may put upon such procedure. The exigency of our public affairs leaves no other alternative from a state of anarchy.

Sixth. You are to give diligent attention to the advice which you may receive from the Continental Congress now sittting at Philadelphia, and we shall esteem it the greatest happiness to have the approbation of our sister colonies in all matters respecting our mode of government, and therefore if your advices from said Congress should not perfectly coincide with these, our instructions respecting the mode of government for this Province, you are to desist from acting any further on that matter until you have our further instructions, anything herein contained to the contrary notwithstanding.

Seventh. That whereas, the commissioned officers in the militia of this Province have generally resigned their commissions and the people have formed themselves into military companies and chosen officers of their respective companies, field officers, &c., notwithstanding all which, it is highly necessary that there be a Captain General to preside over the whole, we therefore instruct you that you endeavor that there be such a Captain General advised to by the Provincial Congress as soon as may be.

Eighth. The foregoing you are to adhere to and religiously observe in all respects, according to the nature of your office, and as the way and means for the recovery and defence of our rights, liberties and privileges.

By order of the Committee,

DAVID BANCROFT, Chairman.

On the 25th of October, a committee consisting of Nathan Baldwin, John Kelso and Ebenezer Lovell, was appointed to see that the merchants and traders of the town offered no goods for sale in violation of the "Solemn League and Covenant."

The Massachusetts Committee of Safety recommended to the Committee of Supplies, the procuring of pork, flour, rice and peas, and depositing the same partly at Worcester, and partly at Concord. They further advised the procuring of all arms and ammunition that could be got from the neighboring Provinces, and also spades, pickaxes, bill-hooks, iron pots, mess-boards, cannon balls, etc.

In Committee of Safety, Nov. 2d, 1774,* it was " voted to procure supplies as soon as may be, and that 200 barrels of pork, 400 barrels of flour, 150 bushels of peas, be deposited at Worcester; also at Concord, 155 barrels of pork, 300 barrels of flour, 50 tierces of rice and 150 bushels of peas."

Jan. 25, 1775, " voted, that all the cannon, mortars, cannon balls and shells, be deposited at the towns of Worcester and Concord in the same proportion that the provisions are deposited."

Feb. 22d, " voted, that Mr. Abram Watson on the arrival of more troops, take possession of the Province arms, now in the college, and send them to Worcester; and also voted that the Province arms now in Boston and Roxbury be removed by Moses Gill, Esq., to Worcester."

March 7, " voted, that watches be kept constantly, at places where the Provincial magazines are kept, and that the clerk write on the subject to Col. Barrett of Concord, Henry Gardner, Esq., of Stowe, and Captain Timothy Bigelow of Worcester, leaving it to them how many the watches shall consist of."

---

*From Journals of the Committee of Safety and of the Committee of Supplies of the Provincial Congress of Massachusetts, 1774,—1775.

April 17. "voted, that all ammunition shall be deposited in nine towns in this Province, viz: Worcester, Lancaster, Concord, Groton, Stoughton, Stowe, Mendon, Leicester and Sudbury."

April 18. "voted, that the town of Worcester, Concord, Stowe and Lancaster be furnished with two iron three-pound cannon, each. That 500 iron pots be deposited at Sudbury, 500 at Concord, and 1000 at Worcester. That 2000 wooden bowls be deposited as are the pots, and the spoons in the same manner, also canteens, two medical chests in Worcester in different parts of the town: 1600 yards of Russia Linen: 1100 tents to be deposited in equal parts in Worcester, Lancaster, Groton, Stowe, Mendon, Leicester and Sudbury."

April 30. "voted, that an order be given to Maj. Timothy Bigelow to have the Province arms, either at Worcester or Concord immediately brought to this town."*

At a town meeting held January 3d, 1775, Timothy Bigelow was chosen Delegate to the Provincial Congress, and a committee comsisting of Nathan Baldwin, David Bancroft and Jonathan Stone was appointed to draw up instructions for him and lay the same before the town at the adjournment of the meeting.

At the adjourned meeting, the Committee submitted the following, which were adopted:

To Mr. Timothy Bigelow,

Sir: At this day of difficulty and trial in general, and in this Province in particular, by means of several acts of the British Parliament whereby we are deprived of the advantages of Civil Government agreeable to the rights, liberties and privileges of Englishmen, the Governor of this Province, invested with a power of making and unmaking many of our officers in such manner as renders our executive courts dangerous to the lives, liberties and properties of all such as

---

*The Committee of Safety were then holding their sessions at Cambridge.

shall oppose the establishment of a despotic government in this Province, and his being made independent of the people of this Province for his salary, we apprehend has such an influence upon his conduct, that we have just ground to fear he will pay more regard to the instructions he may receive from the British Ministry than to the welfare of this Province or the English Constitution of Government.

He has already, (we think wantonly,) dissolved our General Assembly of this Province, and issued writs for calling another, and in an unprecedented manner dissolved said writ before the day on which the said Court was to meet, and no other like to be called that we know of, by these means we being deprived of the advantages of such a General Court or Assembly as the Charter of this Province entitles us to, we are constrained instead thereof, to hold a Provincial Congress agreeable to the recommendation of our late Congress held at Cambridge. Therefore we have made choice of you to represent us in said Congress at this critical and important crisis of our public affairs, when the fate of millions depends upon our wise, cool and prudent conduct; you, we make no doubt, will be duly sensible of the great and important trust reposed in you by us, your constituents, the uncertainty of events may cause many matters to come under your consideration which will require your utmost fortitude, which we cannot give definite instructions upon at this time, but the following we give you as the rule of your conduct respecting the matters hereinafter mentioned, viz:

First. That you endeavor that if the Provincial Congress should meet at Cambridge, agreeable to the recommendation of our late Congress, that they immediately adjourn from Cambridge to some other town in the country at a greater distance from Boston.

Second. That you are very careful in disposing of the public monies, especially that you do not give your consent to extravagant grants if any such should be proposed to be made to any person or persons for their services.

Third. That you endeavor that the members chosen by our late Provincial Congress to sit in a Continental Congress to be holden at Philadelphia in May next, may be instructed as early in their session as possible to obtain the advice of the members thereof, what measures are the most proper for this Province to adopt respecting civil government which we at this time are deprived of. And we determine to rest quietly in this situation, however perplexing, agreeable to the recommendations of our late Continental Congress until the operations of their petition to his Majesty be known, excepting the commencement of hostilities against us should require the adopting a form of civil government for the defence of our lives and properties; and under such exigency you are to conduct yourself accordingly, and endeavor the best form possible be adopted for the support of good order and the liberties of the people which we think must and shall make every servant of the public dependent upon the suffrages of the people for their authority.

NATHAN BALDWIN.
JONATHAN STONE.

At a town meeting held in January, 1775, it was " voted, to recommend to the company of minute men, that they discipline themselves in the military art, until the month of March next, and then the town to give them proper encouragement after that time."

In accordance with the above, at the March meeting it was "voted, that each of the minute men belonging to the town, attending drill one-half day of each week, shall be paid by the town one shilling per man for each one-half days' service, for so many half days as they shall train more than other companies shall do that belong to this town, and all who have enlisted as minute men who do not punctually attend when notified by their commanding officer, shall pay one shilling out of their wages for each and every one-half day of their neglect."

These men were soon called into active service. On the 19th of April, the day of the battle of Lexington, a little before noon, a mounted messenger dashed through the town, with the alarm " to arms! to arms! the war is begun!" His horse covered with foam, and bleeding from the effects of his rider's spurs, fell exhausted near the church; another was procured, and the messenger hurried on with his summons to the field. The bell was rung, cannon were fired, and the minute men, true to their agreement, were ready at a minute's notice, and rallied on the common, where they were paraded by Capt. Timothy Bigelow. After prayer by Rev. Thaddeus Maccarty, at about five o'clock in the afternoon they took up their line of march through Shrewsbury, Northboro, Marlboro, Sudbury, Weston, Waltham, to Watertown, where they arrived the next morning, and after a short halt, proceeded to Cambridge. Capt. Bigelow was soon followed by Capt. Benjamin Flagg, with a company of thirty-one men, and overtook the former at Sudbury. On that 19th of April, 108 men left Worcester to repel British invasion.

The organization of the army which had gathered at Cambridge, was immediately begun. Captain Bigelow was appointed Major in the regiment of which Jonathan Ward was colonel. A greater part of the Worcester men enlisted on the 24th of April, in a company of which Jonas Hubbard, who was 1st Lieutenant of Bigelow's company of minute men, was captain. Many joined other companies in Ward's and Doolittle's regiments, and others still, enlisted in the artillery under Col. Thomas Crafts.

On the day following the battle of Lexington, there arrived in Worcester, a man who was destined to act a leading part in promoting the cause of the people, in Worcester. The bold and resolute course adopted by Mr. Isaiah Thomas, proprietor of the Massachusetts Spy, had rendered him obnoxious to the British authorities. With the assistance of a few of the patriots, he succeeded in removing a portion of his presses and types from Boston and reached Worcester on the 20th, and on the third day of May, he issued the first number of the Spy printed in Worcester. His utterances through its columns were powerful in sustaining the cause in the heart of the Province.

Five days after the battle of Lexington, the Hon. John Hancock, on his journey to Philadelphia to attend the Continental Congress, was detained in this town two days awaiting the arrival of his colleagues, delegates from Massachusetts, and the attendance of an escort. While here, he sent a letter to the President of the Provincial Congress at Watertown, giving information of the arrival of a packet at New York, with dispatches for General Gage, and recommended that care be taken to intercept the same. He also sent the following letters to the Committee of Safety:

WORCESTER, 24th April, 1775, Monday Evening.

"GENTLEMEN:—Mr. S. Adams and myself, just arrived here, find no intelligence from you and no guard. We just hear an express has just passed through this place to you from New York, informing that administration is bent upon pushing matters; and that four regiments are expected there. How are we to proceed? Where are our brethren? Surely we ought to be supported. I had rather be with you; and, at present, am fully determined to be with you before I proceed. I beg, by the return of this express, to hear from you; and pray furnish us with depositions of the conduct of the troops, the certainty of their firing first, and every circumstance relative to the conduct of the troops, from the 19th instant to this time, that we may be able to give some account of matters as we proceed, and especially at Philadelphia. Also I beg you would order your Secretary to make out an account of your proceedings since what has taken place; what your plan is; what prisoners we have, and what they have of ours; who of note was killed on both sides; who commands our forces, &c."

"Are our men in good spirits? For God's sake, do not suffer the spirit to subside until they have perfected the reduction of our enemies. Boston *must* be entered; the troops *must* be sent away, or [blank] Our friends are valuable but our Country must be saved. I have an interest in that town; what can be the enjoyment of that to me, if I am obliged to hold it at the will of General Gage, or any one else? I doubt not your vigilance, your fortitude and resolution. Do let us know how you proceed. We must have the castle. The ships must be [blank] Stop up the harbor against large vessels coming. You know better what to do than I can point out. Where is Mr.

Cushing? Are Mr. Paine and Mr. John Adams to be with us? What are we to depend upon? We travel rather as deserters, which I will not submit to. I will return and join you, if I cannot travel in reputation. I wish to hear from you. Pray spend a thought upon our situation. I will not detain this man, as I want much to hear from you. How goes on the Congress? Who is your president? Are the members hearty? Pray remember Mr. S. Adams and myself to all friends. God be with you.

I am, gentlemen, your faithful and hearty countryman.

JOHN HANCOCK."

" To the gentlemen Committee of Safety."

" WORCESTER, April 24, 1775.

" GENTLEMEN:—From a conviction of your disposition to promote the general good, I take the freedom to request your countenance and good offices in favor of Mr. Edward Crafts,* of this place, that he may be appointed to the command of a company. I know him well; he is capable. I beg your attention to this. It will give great satisfaction to Mr. Adams and myself, and to the people of this county: do gratify us. I also beg leave, you would recommend to the notice of General Heath, in my name. Mr. Nathaniel Nazro, of this town, who is desirous of being noticed in the army. He is lively, active and capable. My respects to Heath and all friends. Pray General Heath to take notice of this recommendation. God bless you. Adieu.

I am your real friend.

JOHN HANCOCK."

" To the Committee of Safety."

" WORCESTER, April 26, 1775.

" GENTLEMEN:—Having had the honor to command the Cadet company at Boston, and knowing the ability of those who composed that corps, I cannot withhhold mentioning, and recommending to the notice of you and the general officers, Mr. John Smith and Mr. John Avery, two excellent good soldiers and gentlemen, who will advance the reputation of the Province in that department of command where they may be placed. I therefore most strongly recommend them, and earnestly pray they may be noticed. I will be answerable for their conduct. There are several other gentlemen of that corps, who may be useful, particularly Mr. Brent and Mr. Cunningham. Do notice Messrs Smith and Avery.* They will be useful. I set out to-morrow

---

*Messrs. Smith and Crafts received Commissions and proved valuable officers.

morning. God bless you. Why don't you send to Mr. Crafts. Pray improve him. He is a good man, and one on whom you may depend. Don't miss him.

I am your real friend,

JOHN HANCOCK."

"To the Committee of Safety."

After the battle of Lexington, the Committees of the town turned their attention to the "internal enemies," as may be seen from the following papers* issued by them.

"WORCESTER, May 8, 1775.

The committee appointed by the inhabitants of the town to take into their consideration what is requisite to be done with a number of people who have shown themselves disaffected to their country, do report: That in their humble opinion, William Campbell, as he has broken through his engagements with the fathers of the people, and presumed to go out of the town and Province, before the resolves of the Provincial Congress were known, in order to injure the good people of this place, and has been, and by his conduct still appears to be an inveterate enemy to the rights and privileges of this country, notwithstanding his declarations to the contrary, that he should be sent to Watertown or Cambridge, to be dealt with as the Honorable Congress, or the Commander-in-Chief shall think necessary, it being judged highly improper that he should tarry any longer in this town.

That Jacob Stearns, Samuel Paine, Micah Johnson, David Moore, Samuel Brooks, Cornelius Stowell, Capt. Curtis, Jacob Chamberlain, James Hart, Joseph Clark, Capt. Rice, Joseph Blair, Joshua Johnson, Adam Walker, Capt. Samuel Mower, Samuel Moore, Dr. Willard, Nathan Patch and Lieut. John Mower, as every person in this day of distress, who is not an enemy of his country, should aid and assist all in their power to extricate it out of its present difficulties, that the above gentlemen have an opportunity offered them of retrieving the good opinion of their fellow townsmen, by heartily consenting to join the American troops, or find others in their stead, otherwise they must be looked upon as unworthy of the further confidence of their fellow countrymen, and willing to join an unlawful banditti to murder and ravage. By order of the Committee."

This Report was accepted:

---

*From original papers in possession of the American Antiquarian Society.

"WORCESTER, May 17, 1775.

To GARDNER CHANDLER, Esq.,

Sir: The Committee of Correspondence for the town of Worcescester, have resolved that David Moore, Micah Johnson, Micah Johnson, Jr., Samuel Moore, Samuel Moore, Jr., Jacob Chamberlain, John and Thad., John Curtis, William Curtis, Joseph Blair, Joshua Johnson, Cornelius Stowell, P. Goulding, C. and N. Chandler, Nahum Willard, Andrew Duncan, John Mower, Elisha Smith, Joseph Clark, Adam Walker, Nathan Patch, Nathaniel Adams, Isaac Barnard, Timothy Paine, Samuel Paine, Samuel Moore and Noah Harris, meet said Committee Monday next, at nine o'clock in the forenoon, at the house of Mrs. Sternes,* in Worcester, with their arms and ammunition. You are desired by said Committee to notify said persons thereof.

By order of the Committee,

WILLIAM YOUNG."

"WORCESTER, May 22d, 1775.

In Committee of Correspondence, determined that the persons herein named† be, agreeable to Resolution of Provincial Congress, forthwith disarmed, and that they do not depart the town without a permit in writing from the Committee of Correspondence of the town of Worcester, or such person or persons as they shall appoint for that purpose; and that if any of said persons shall be so daring as to violate this resolve, and depart the town contrary thereto, that he or they be immediately advertised in the public papers, and when brought back, be dealt with as shall be thought proper; and that for the future they desist from meeting together in larger or smaller companies.

N. B. It is to be understood that we do not mean to prevent any persons from laboring on their own land in this or the adjacent towns.

Per Order,

WM. YOUNG."

While these things were transpiring at home, the Worcester soldiers were taking an important part in the investment of Boston. Capt. Hubbard's company in Col. Ward's Regiment was stationed for about six weeks near Charles River in Cambridge, opposite the

---

*King's Arms Tavern.
†Names as in preceding Document.

Colleges; after which, until the latter part of July, they were at Fort No. 2, which they assisted in constructing; they were then ordered to Dorchester, where they remained until their term of service expired. At the Battle of Bunker Hill, the regiment was marched down within a little over a mile of the scene of action, when they were ordered to halt. Half of the regiment was ordered to remain on the ground they occupied for further orders; in this part was Capt. Hubbard's company; the other half advanced and took part in the engagement. After occupying the ground for an hour or two, that part of the regiment which included Hubbard's company, were ordered to advance, and marched within about a mile of the hill, where they met soldiers from the other part of the regiment returning from the battle, under a cannonade from the British. Col. Ward ordered a halt, and the regiment remained near the ground until the next morning, when they returned to Fort No. 2.

At a town meeting held May 22, 1775, Mr. David Bancroft was chosen Delegate to the Provincial Congress to be convened in Watertown the 31st of May, and continue in said office six months and no longer. A committee consisting of William Young, Josiah Pierce, Nathan Baldwin, Jonathan Stone, and Samuel Curtis, was chosen to draw up instructions to be observed by him, and report at an adjourned meeting, at which the following were adopted unanimously.

To Mr. DAVID BANCROFT,

SIR: The Town of Worcester having chosen you their Delegate to represent them in the Provincial Congress, to be convened and held at Watertown upon the 31st of May inst. and so *de die in diem* during their session and sessions, for six months from the said 31st of May and no longer; and notwithstanding the high opinion we have of your enlightened wisdom and fortitude, think it our duty, to give you our particular instructions, relative to some matters that may come under your consideration; and when anything extraordinary of a public nature occurs, that concerns your duty as our Representative, we enjoin upon you that you take our further particular instructions upon the matter if in your power, especially at this time when a corrupt and despotic ministry, with a wink or a nod, rules both the King and Parliament of Great Britain with such absolute sway, that they are but a mere nose of wax, turned and moulded any and every way, to answer despotic purposes, overthrow the English Constitution of Government and plunder the Americans of both liberty and property. From hence our Charter nullified; our Governor made despotic and independent of the people; our Judges of our Courts dependent upon the King for both place and pay; Jurors to be packed by a dependent Sheriff; a law purporting for the King's officers, if they please, to murder the King's subjects in this Province with impunity; the port and harbor of Boston blocked up, and our trade stopped until we shall pay for tea we know not how much, and destroyed by we know not whom, (and if we do not comply and pay for said tea, then all the wharves, docks, quays, landing places and shores within the port and harbor of Boston are forfeited unto the hand, and are to be at the disposal of his present Majesty and his successors forever;) the town of Boston reduced to military government, the Governor of this Province sending out troops into the country frequently, who have robbed and plundered public stores, magazines and so forth, and destroyed private property, and to complete the scene have murdered and butchered a great number of our peaceable, quiet inhabitants, and loyal subjects of his Majesty; our Legislative authority according to charter destroyed, and we driven to the necessity instead thereof to hold a Congress; and as though spiritual ruin was designed against us as well as temporal, the Romish religion is established in the largest government upon the continent; civil government, the former security of life and property, we are deprived of, and under the disagreeable necessity of taking up arms and defending ourselves against Britons who ought to join with us in the defence of our lives, rights, liberties and the English Constitution, the only safe basis of his Majesty's throne. These are but a part of the acts of that Legislature that claims a right to make laws that are binding upon us in all cases whatever. Under these accumulated oppressions, and tyrannical acts of the British Parliament, it behooves you to steer clear of those rocks that have dashed the constitutional liberties of our fellow subjects in Great Britain, and that threaten us in America. The millions upon millions of the national debt hath arisen (as we think, not by misfortune but) by exorbitant grants to place-men and pensioners. You are therefore in all grants of the public money to be especially careful that no more is given to any person for his services than an adequate pay for the same, and that no person be allowed to live in luxury and idleness or become opulently rich, at the public expense. There is nothing in a well ordered government that requires it; and in whatever community it is allowed, they are raising such another tribe of tyrants to destroy themselves, as we are now fighting against. This requires nothing for its illustration but to take a retrospective view of the conduct of some persons in this town, as well as other parts of the Province. God grant that this country may never produce any more such ingrates. The difficulties we labor under for want of an established civil government, necessitates us to enjoin it upon you, that you endeavor that advice of the Grand Continental Congress be obtained upon that matter, and that we have such a form of government established as that every officer in it be dependent upon the suffrages of the people for their place and pay. And as Gen. Gage, commander-in-chief of his Majesty's forces in America, hath since he has been in Boston, sent out his troops into the country, who have robbed plundered and murdered a number of his Majesty's loyal subjects, and by fraud disarmed the inhabitants of Boston, and by breach of solemn contract detained some of them prisoners in Boston, and been guilty of such conduct, as is not only unchristian and derogatory to the character of a good soldier, but would be a disgrace to a savage,—you are therefore, as far as is consistent with the nature of your office, to give all the aid and assistance in your power, toward subjecting him and the army under his command, and recovering the property both public and private, that they have unjustly taken away, and that he and the murderers under his command, may be brought to condign punishment, and that the estates of our domestic enemies may be secured for the public use. You are also to endeavor, that proper measures be taken, to supply this Colony with arms, ammunition, and all war-like stores necessary for defence, and to take proper measures for keeping up harmony and union, with all our sister Colonies.

In the spring of 1775, captives from the British army began to arrive, and during the remainder of the year the jail was filled to its utmost capacity with prisoners of war. Many were put out to service among the inhabitants of the town on parole, when proper persons appeared to hire them; those hiring them being required to obtain a certificate from the Committee of Safety recommending them as friendly to the American cause, and to give a receipt to the Sheriff, at the same time engaging to return the prisoners whenever required.

In May, the Continental Congress provided for the removal of the poor of Boston, and a number were supported here.

The Selectmen, were required to furnish blankets for the soldiers of the town, which was promptly done. In June, a requisition was made for 30 muskets and bayonest, which were furnished, also $2\frac{1}{2}$ barrels of powder.

In September, the march through the wilderness to Quebec, and the subsequent attack on that fortress, was conceived, and in that most disastrous expedition, Worcester was represented; her soldiers showing themselves possessed of a true soldierly spirit and undaunted heroism. Major Bigelow, Capt. Hubbard, and twelve soldiers of this town took part in the attack on the fortifications, on the last day of the year 1775. Capt. Hubbard was mortally wounded, and refusing to be moved, perished in the violent snow storm which was raging at that time; two others were killed, and Major Bigelow and the remainder were taken prisoners and confined nearly a year, when they were exchanged.

On the 10th of July, Mr. David Bancroft was chosen Representative, and a committee consisting of Nathan Baldwin, David Bigelow, Asa Moore, John Nazro and Samuel Curtis, was chosen to report instructions at the adjournment, on the 14th. At this adjourned meeting, Mr. Joshua Bigelow was chosen as colleague with Mr. Bancroft.

The committee reported the following instructions which were adopted.

To Mr. DAVID BANCROFT and Mr. JOSHUA BIGELOW, Representatives for the Town of Worcester,

GENTLEMEN: We, your constitutents, having invested you with authority to act for us in a legislative capacity, and as this is a power you received from us, to use and exercise for our safety and benefit, you are therefore accountable to us for all your conduct in said office, and under indispensible obligation to observe and obey such instructions as we may at this or any other time give you respecting the discharging the duties of your office, so long as you remain.

At this crisis, when the British Parliament, regardless of our natural and constitutional rights, has annihilated our Charter and demanded of us an implicit obedience to their acts and laws in all cases whatsoever; and to reduce us to subjection to their mandates, His Majesty has appointed Thomas Gage, Esq., Governor of this Colony, with an army under his command, who has actually robbed and murdered a great number of his Majesty's loyal subjects, and by proclamation has established martial law to be the only rule of government in this Colony, and imprisoned a great number of the peaceable inhabitants of the town of Boston, and has been guilty of many other actions that are a disgrace to humanity; and as we have good reason to believe that the Deputy Governor is aiding and assisting in these cruel operations, we highly approve the advice of the Honorable Continental Congress, viz: to consider the Governor and Deputy Governor as absent, and for the House of Representatives to choose a Council, and that Council to act as Governor until his Majesty shall please to appoint a Governor and Deputy Governor, that shall act agreeable to the Charter of this Colony, or it be otherwise ordered by the authority of the United Colonies of North America.

The accumulated difficulties that we labor under at this time, added to those passions that too often lead men into error, makes the task of a virtuous representative truly arduous. An inordinate desire of riches and power has induced some men to barter the rights and liberties of their constitutents for a lucrative office, or some post of command; from hence we think that the national debt hath, the greatest part of it arisen, and the liberties of Englishmen invaded, for by the accounts we often receive, the members of the British Parliament are very generous in granting pensions and places to each other. You are therefore to endeavor that none be elected Councillors but persons of established character for probity and virtue, and as it is expected that they will appoint executive officers, and may perhaps appoint each other into the most lucrative offices, and continue the fees as heretofore established, or refuse to give their concurrence to a more equitable law for the regulation of that matter, you are to use your influence that the legislative and executive authority be kept in separate hands as much as may be; for we look upon it as incompatible with the privileges of equity for men to appoint themselves into executive offices, as it would be for a plaintiff that had sued for a *quantum meruit* to sit upon the jury and determine how much he should recover of the defendant. You are therefore to endeavor that an act be passed, that whenever any member of the Legislature be appointed to accept of an executive office, he shall be debarred a seat in the Legislature until he shall be re-chosen, and that his constituents shall be forthwith served with a precept to choose some suitable person to represent them. And whereas, executive officers being persons in good repute among those whom their respective offices immediately concern, and it is of great utility in civil society as it greatly facilitates subordination, you are to endeavor that no person be appointed to the office of a Judge of the Probate, or Register in the Probate Office, or a Justice of the Court of Common Pleas, or a Clerk of the same, or Clerk of the Court of General Sessions of the Peace, or Sheriff of the County, before he or they are recommended to be suitable persons for their respective offices by a vote of the inhabitants of the major part of the towns of the County in which they are to exercise their offices. We also further instruct you to endeavor that we have Executive Courts established, that criminals may be punished in due form of law, and that creditors may recover their just debts; but as the long discontinuance of Courts of Justice and other circumstances have stopped the circulation of money among us, to enter precipitately into civil actions might be attended with bad consequences to the public, you are therefore directed to endeavor that such a limited time be set for the commencement of civil actions, as shall be the most impartial between debtors and creditors and best serve the public.

And whereas, Gen. Gage has broken faith with the inhabitants of Boston by retaining many of them and their effects there, and sending out the poor only; and as there are a number of persons inimical to the liberties of this country who have taken refuge in Boston and left their families and considerable interests in the country, you are to endeavor that some method be provided that those families may be sent to Boston, and that their estates be appropriated to the public use; the law of restoration and self preservation suggests it, and there is no breach of faith in doing it. In all other matters that may come under your consideration adhere strictly to our constitutional rights, and that you may be prospered and acquit yourself with honor is our fervent prayer.

The summary manner in which the Committees dealt with the tories at home, may be seen by the following from the Spy of August 30, 1775.

"Dr. Nahum Willard of this town, having at divers times and in the presence of sundry persons, most scandalously aspersed the character of some, and the proceedings of the whole of the Continental and Provincial Congresses, the Selectmen of this Town, and the Committee of Correspondence in general, the good people of this town from a knowledge of his character, for some time passed it unnoticed, from an apprehension that his character was so well established for a retailer of falsehoods as to render him incapable of doing any public injury; but from the preverseness of his vile heart whereby he persisted in his wickedness, they were apprehensive he might be capable of doing some hurt in the neighboring towns, which he often frequented, and where his character perhaps may not be so well known, and from an apprehension the inhabitants of this town might hazard the imputation of having deserted the glorious cause for which this continent is now contending, in suffering such an offender to escape with impunity, did on the 21st inst., summon said Willard to appear before them in the presence of the Selectmen and some of the Committee of Correspondence, when witnesses were produced in support of the charges alleged against him, which were fully proved and committed to writing and deposited in the hands of the Selectmen, (open to inspection,) the witnesses being ready to make oath to the same.

A committee was then chosen to consider the best methods for a further procedure with said Willard. They reported that said Willard should have tendered to him a paper they had drawn up, containing a confession of his notorious scandals and falsehoods, (without mentioning a word of his promising a reformation, as they would be very sorry to be the means of his adding to his falsehoods;) this paper if he believed to be true, he was to sign that evening, and as it was late, to prevent disorder, he was next morning to read it in such public parts of the town as the company desired, with which he complied.

There was another scandalous aspersion upon the guard that conducted the prisoners from hence to Springfield, wherein he asserted he was told they used them extremely cruel, frequently pricking them with their bayonets; he was often called upon to name his author, and as often refused it, until the day of general enquiry, when he laid it upon a person four miles off, who has since declared he never told him so, nor ever heard of it before; this is only mentioned to take off any bad impression that might be made, to the prejudice of the gentlemen who conducted this matter, whose character is so well known here, especially for humanity, that it never affected it in this place. But as this matter was not of so public a nature, it was thought most advisable the persons who had suffered should do themselves justice; an apprehension that they would, it is supposed, has caused the Doctor's flight, without the least regret of any of the inhabitants except the tory gentry."

CONFESSION OF DR. WILLARD.

"Whereas I, the subscriber, have from the perverseness of my wicked heart, maliciously and scandalously abused the characters and proceedings of the Continental and Provincial Congresses, the Selectmen of the town, and the Committees of Correspondence in general; I do hereby declare, that at the time of my doing it, I knew the said abuses to be the most scandalous falsehoods, and that I did it for the sole purpose of abusing those bodies of men, and affronting my townsmen, and all the friends of liberty, throughout the continent, being now fully sensible of my wickedness and notorious falsehoods, humbly beg pardon of those worthy characters I have so scandalously abused, and of my countrymen in general, and desire this confession of mine may be printed in the American Oracle of Liberty, for three weeks successively."

Signed, NAHUM WILLARD.

Attest,

BENJAMIN FLAGG, JOSIAH PIERCE,
JONATHAN STONE, DAVID BIGELOW.
SAMUEL MILLER,

CHAPTER IV.

Col. Ward's Regiment petition the General Assembly concerning the tories—The tories address Gen. Gage on his departure for England—Clark Carpenter committed to jail for assisting a prisoner of war to escape—He petitions the General Court and Committee of Safety for enlargement—Town voted to sustain the measure if Congress should declare the American Colonies independent—Troops raised and forwarded to Boston, New York and Canada—The price of Bohea Tea and other articles fixed by Congress.

In September, 1775, the officers and men of Col. Ward's regiment at Dorchester, which regiment was composed mostly of men from Worcester county, petitioned the General Assembly then in session at Watertown, that the internal enemies or royalists, who had fled to Boston, might be prohibited from returning to their former habitations, and if they attempted to return that they might be severely dealt with.

PETITION.

"To the Honorable Board of Councillors and House of Representatives of the Province of Massachusetts Bay, in the General Assembly now sitting at Watertown:

The memorial of the company of foot, raised in the town of Worcester, and now in the Continental army, in the regiment whereof Jonathan Ward, Esq., is Colonel, together with the principal part of said regiment, being raised out of the county of Worcester, humbly sheweth:—

That the said town and county, has been intolerably infested with a cruel and merciless set of tories, who have exerted all their wit, sophistry and influence, to proselyte slaves to the supreme legislative power of the British Parliament, and to disconcert every method used by the wise and zealous friends of a free, happy and most noble constitution of the Empire, and discovered a most merciless, inimical temper toward our Provincial and Colony Charters, styling the sons of freedom or friends to the constitution, as rebels and traitors, and menacing death and cruel tortures as their just and remediless portion.

That when the bloody era commenced, and the brave appeared in arms to defend their invaluable rights against troops, formed, posted, and ordered to massacre all that would not submit to their merciless decrees; and all America with one heart and voice, cordially united to take up arms as their dernier resort for their defence, then these wretches trembled, some confessed, and like vermin crawling among the roots of vegetables, endeavoring to secrete themselves, while they are a nuisance to the cause of justice and judgment; or in sheep's clothing secretly watching for prey to gratify their voracious appetites, or availing themselves of the good opinion of the prudent, ascend into places of power and profit, and rendered capable of acting their predecessor Judas' part, when opportunity favors their designs, and betray the good cause with "all hail," and a hypocritical kiss.

That others fled to Boston, there to advise and act as open and avowed enemies to their brethren; encouraging the disheartened and chagrined troops to all merciless acts of violence and bloody scenes; stimulating the British Ministry and all the tools of tyranny to pursue their bloody decrees with all vengeance upon us, by which means, in our humble opinion they have forfeited all right to American property, and even their lives with every aggravation of guilt, as did ever a bloody set of merciless robbers, or desperate pirates.

That as some of these vermin, or worse, emissaries of tyranny, are crawling out of Boston to their forfeited seats in Worcester, there is reason to suspect, that either their expectations fail, and therefore they would gladly return to their former seats and profits, until a more favorable opportunity presents to carry their evil machinations into execution, or, they are contriving, by degrees, to slide back to their seats, and there avail themselves of the good opinion of the people, in order to play their parts, to divide and subdivide, or by some method weaken our union, or to form some diabolical plan for the Ministry to save the supremacy of Parliament, under some soft, sophistical, reconciliatory terms.

Wherefore, we, your humble memorialists, entreat your honors not to suffer any of those who return, however humble and penitent they may appear, to go at large, or return to their former seats, or even to be so far favored as to be confined within the limits of Worcester, but treat them as they deserve, enemies in a superlative degree; confine them close, and render them incapable of doing harm, or return them to Boston their favorite asylum.

Your Honor's petitioners can but flatter themselves with a most sanguine expectation of this so rational request being fully granted, especially as we are risking our lives in our country's cause; it must greatly dishearten us to hear our most notorious enemies are tolerated and winked at, while on the other hand we find no necessity to pray to our commander-in-chief for a detachment to apprehend and confine enemies who are secured properly by our civil fathers under whose jurisdiction they appear; and thus encouraged as in duty bound, shall ever pray.

DORCHESTER, Sept. 27, 1775.

"The gentlemen who were driven from their habitations in the country, to the town of Boston" issued an address to Gen. Gage on his departure for England, in the most loyal terms.

"To his Excellency, Thomas Gage, Esqr., Captain General and Commander-in-Chief in and over his Majesty's Province of Massachusetts Bay in New England.

May it please your Excellency: When we reflect upon the surprising effects of that enthusiasm and infatuation which are so generally prevalent in the country, and the variety of dangers to which the loyal and obedient have been exposed, we feel the most grateful sensations towards your Excellency, and are anxious to acknowledge our obligations to your wisdom and prudence. We consider ourselves indebted to you for protection from the lawless fury and unbridled violence of our countrymen, and had not events taken place beyond what human wisdom could foresee, and contrary to any human calculation upon rational principles, we might in all probability have been further indebted to your Excellency for a reconciliation of the unhappy differences that subsist, and a restoration to harmony, happiness and peace.

It is with regret we think of your Excellency's departure from this Province, but we are relieved in some degree, by a consideration of the very important services you will render this country, by a just representation of its present state at the Court of Great Britain; by the confidence we repose in the abilities of your successor to the civil and military command, the hopes of your speedy return, and the anticipation of an establishment of the rightful supremacy of Parliament over this part of his Majesty's dominions. Justly meriting and possessed of the esteem and applause of the virtuous and good, happy in the pleasing reflections of an approving conscience, and blessed with the gracious plaudits of the best of Kings, your opportunities will be equal to the inclination you have ever discovered, to restore and settle on the most lasting basis, that union of the interests of Great Britain and the Colonies, so indispensably necessary to the happiness of both.

We sincerely lament that the number who have dared to stem the torrent of rebellion and sedition in this Province is so small, but we trust that the cordial thanks of even a few, (who have fled from oppression, who have sacrificed their properties and every domestic enjoyment, and are now ready to risk their lives to manifest their loyalty to the best of sovereigns,) will not be unacceptable to your Excellency.

Be pleased, sir, to accept the ardent wishes of these few faithful and grateful subjects, that your voyage may be prosperous and agreeable, and that your unwearied endeavors for the public service may be crowned with success.

Boston, Oct. 7, 1775."

Seventy-six royalists signed this address, among whom were the following, who had fled from Worcester: James Putnam, Samuel Paine, Adam Walker, William Campbell, John Chandler, Nathaniel Chandler, William Chandler, James Putnam, Jr.

Gen. Gage replied, acknowledging the steady attachment they had always shown to the true interests of their King and Country in the worst of times, and assured them that his successor would afford them every favor and protection.

On the 20th of September, Mr. Clark Chandler was charged by the Committee of Correspondence with having in the month of June, assisted one Budd, a prisoner of war in escaping, in violation of the said prisoner's parole of honor, of having spent the summer in Boston and elsewhere with the enemies of America, also of being an enemy to his country; and he was committed to jail in Worcester, and kept in close confinement, his relatives being allowed to furnish him with such necessaries as he stood in need of.

On the 3d of October, he petitioned the Council and House of Representatives for enlargement from close confinement, setting forth that in the month of June he went from Worcester, his place of abode, to Newport, where he went on board one of his Majesty's vessels in which he obtained a passage to Boston, designing to sail from thence to Quebec, where he proposed to reside and engage in trade. Accordingly after a short stop in Boston he sailed for Annapolis in Nova Scotia, having had the misfortune to be cast away, and hearing discouraging reports of the state of trade in Quebec, he determined to return to his home in Worcester, and accordingly returned to Boston, where he arrived on the 28th day of August, and after staying in that town 21 days, he went by water to Newport, from whence he returned to his home in Worcester, arriving on the 20th of September, and considering the situation of public affairs, and being sensible that he had rendered himself justly suspected as an enemy to his country, he voluntarily surrendered himself to the Committee of Correspondence, by whom he was closely confined, to the great detriment of his health, and compelled to endure the nauseous stench of a jail crowded with prisoners taken from the enemy; he therefore petitioned that he might be allowed to walk and breathe in a wholesome air, within such limits and under such bonds and obligations as the Council and House might prescribe.

The petition was referred by the Council to the Committee of Correspondence for the town, they being the authorities who imprisoned him, and who were cognizant of the crimes laid to his charge.

On the 21st of November he sent a lengthy statement and petition to the Committee, which was as follows:

[From MSS. in possession of American Antiquarian Society.]

To the Committee of Correspondence for the town of Worcester: The address, memorial and petition of Clark Chandler, a prisoner in close confinement, humbly showeth,—

That in consequence of his own imprudent and misjudged conduct, he has been more than two months without the least prospect of a trial upon the merits of his case, subjected to endure the accumulated distresses resulting from a total deprivation of liberty, and the inclemencies of a jail imprisonment. He complains of nothing that is past, nor has he the most distant wish to elude an impartial examination, the consequent decisions of justice, or the full demands of the public; confiding in the rectitude and humanity of his countrymen, the inhabitants of his native town, he cheerfully resigned himself into their hands, and acquiesced in his destination to the severities of a jail imprisonment. In this situation he must have been wanting to himself, regardless of a primary law, the great law of self-preservation, implanted by the finger of God in the heart of all his creatures, whose happiness was the benevolent design that gave being to the universe, not to be meditating some means consistent with the safety of the community, to extricate himself from almost intolerable scenes of suffering, to obtain a partial restoration to freedom, and a blessing common to the brute creation, the privilege of breathing an wholesome and pure air. Surely it must be crimes of the blackest dye, a necessity for the general good, that shall deny to an Englishman, under a free government, these common enjoyments. On these principles, from the advice of his friends, your memorialist was induced to address the lenity and justice of the Honorable Council of this Province, for his relief and the public security, but as his commitment was not by this body, they could not with any propriety sustain his petition, being no ways privy to the suspicions he was under, or the crimes laid to his charge. This transaction, and the reason of the thing, necessarily refer him back to the authority of this town, to the authority that confined him, and who alone can, with any propriety grant him enlargement. Your petitioner has no where else to resort; the town are acquainted with his conduct, with the alleviating and aggravating circumstances attending it. He relies on your recollection, repairs to your goodness, and appeals to your justice. If his conduct has been such as to deny him relief at this bar his misery for the present is perfectly complete. He is now pleading for liberty, without which existence is a burden, and which you all professedly hold dearer than life. Be pleased therefore to hear him with patience, to determine with caution, and consider with attention. His cause is before a people where liberty is sure of finding protection and support, where innocency can never want friends and guardians. It would be injurious to your character, a reflection on your humanity and your justice, to suppose that you would wish your petitioner to suffer out of proportion to the demands of his crimes, that you would not rather spare the unfortunate and afflicted, than to add keenness to anguish, and make wretchedness more wretched.

It is only necessary therefore to convince you he is entitled to indulgence, that the public will be safe, and his enlargement is granted. He does not ask a restoration to your confidence, for this he has no pretensions. He does not solicit an acquittal from the charges he is under; he acknowledges his imprudence, censures his own conduct, confesses the justness of your suspicions, and tenders sufficient securities. He asks not a general enlargement, he asks not what every Englishman has a right to demand, be his crime ever so great, his villiany ever so atrocious, either a trial by his peers, a general bailment, or full discharge. Your petitioner asks only to exchange the walls of a loathsome prison, for the limits of this, or a neighboring town, to go from the custody of a jailor to the care of a sufficient number of responsible bondsmen. He tenders you sureties for his continuing within prescribed boundaries, for his unexceptionable behavior, and for his appearance whenever demanded. It is only on these conditions he prays for enlargement. That this will be safe, he even dares to appeal to precedents, and his past behavior, bad as it is, which will give some little security for his future conduct. It is always unfortunate when a man must vindicate his innocency against general presumptions, unfortunate, because however faultless, it is seldom in his power. Be pleased to recollect circumstances, and listen candidly to the suggestions of truth; if your memorialist is guilty, he is criminal but in degree, and the actions of his life ought to mark the degree of that guilt. Two years have not yet elapsed since your own unsolicited suffrages bore testimony to the goodness of his heart in a political view. It is since that period that he has lost your confidence, and exposed himself to the resentments of those with whom he was wont to live in mutual good friendship, familiarity and affection; unhappily about six months since in the distresses of the times, in the differences of opinions, in the variety of prospects, in the uncertainty of events, in the stagnation of trade, at a time when some anticipated, and many were fearful of the worst of consequences, seduced by example, and allured by prospects of emolument, in the indiscretions and spirits of youth, he foolishly and imprudently left Worcester, and found his way into the place garrisoned by your enemies, but at the same time inhabited by many of your best friends. It was not to give information, but purely from a motive of procuring trade. It was not to take arms in opposition to the country, as the event sufficiently proves. He defies his greatest enemy, man, woman or child, he challenges the world to prove that he did one single act there, inimical to the public, but on the contrary, such was his conduct, as in some measure, to render him obnoxious to government, and to expose him to its displeasure. That your memorialist was pushing for trade, is apparent from facts. It is matter of notoriety, from the discouragements of a shipwreck, from the bad prospects of trade either at Annapolis or Canada, he returned to Boston, and embraced the first opportunity to recover his native town. Simply being in this devoted town, was deserving neither of praise or of blame. The criminality of an action depends entirely on its motive and its consequences. Is there any evidence that your memorialist either designed, or did an injury to the cause you are supporting? May not his views have been innocent, he means with respect to the public? Is not the presumption always in favor of innocence until guilt is proved? Is not the best construction always to be put? By what then consists the great guilt of your memorialist? It is said in repairing to Boston contrary to restrictions, and in the seduction of one Budd a prisoner upon parole, and assisting him in his escape. The former of these charges he frankly confesses, and certainly it can never be justified, but it is rather a fault in morality than a crime in politics, for which he must answer to God and his own conscience. That your petitioner was previously knowing to Budd's going off is not to be denied, but that he either persuaded him to it, or assisted him in it, is certainly false ; you will consider the weight of a person's evidence, if he has forfeited his word and his honor, whether he is entitled to full credit, whether when retaken he would not naturally endeavor to obtain favor, and exculpate himself by placing his crimes to the account of another; certainly he who excuses at the expense of his companion is very suspicious.

Did the misfortunes of your petitioner stop here, his case would be less difficult. The peculiar circumstances attendant upon the attempted escape of another prisoner has its perplexities. But are misfortunes a substitute for evidence? Will not the sufferings of your petitioner suffice that he must be made to bear the crimes of every offender? Can innocency be safe, or villainy in danger, if conviction rests upon the word of a confessed liar? Which of his two stories is true, is worthy of belief? One is from necessity false. If you are satisfied that he lies, that he is not to be regarded in his last account, is the first entitled to your credit? Would your memorialist have hazarded a token, not only known to his confidents, but to the whole country? What sufficient motive could have induced him to run such a risk and to part with his money; if he is not to be credited, where is the evidence? Your petitioner asserts that he was ignorant of the matter that the money and the seal were stolen, and that he complained of it in time. If he is now to be convicted on a matter of evidence, that would fix upon a person of a different character not the slightest suspicion, where is the equality and impartiality of that improved constitution, that knows of no difference between any of its subjects? If one man's crimes cannot be proved by evidence consistent with his innocence, can another's be fixed by proof incompatible with guilt? If this is the case, innocency is unsafe, and the fences and barriers against vice are all prostrate. You will remember, gentlemen, that the first examination of the witness was officious, sudden, upon surprise in the perturbation of heart, where were many leading questions asked, and corresponding answers given. That his other examinations were upon recollection, coolly, before authority, after being solemnly cautioned to declare the truth, and that he resolutely persists in the same story. Is not this attended with the best characteristics of truth? If it does not afford some positive proof in favor, does it not take off the force of his first assertion, and leave your petitioner where it found him, and of course no objection to an enlargement. Your memorialist repeats it, his confinement is not for punishment, but for safe custody. He has had no trial, no opportunity for a defence, nor any judgment against him, specifying his crime, its punishment, its nature, degree and duration. And it is unreasonable to suffer the penalties of a violation, before the law has pronounced him a transgressor. But even admitting that a punishment does not necessarily suppose a transgression, and a judgment of law, it certainly has for its object the reformation of the offender and the terror of others. When these two ends are effected, all the ends of society are answered. With respect to the first, after past experience, after suffering that complicated train of evils that have flowed from his misjudged measures, after a conviction of error from feeling its bitter consequences, after drinking largely of the wormwood and the gall, after being driven and tossed about in anxiety and distress, from prospect to disappointment, from disappointment to despair, from Worcester to Boston, from Boston, in the perils, dangers and wrecks of the sea, to Annapolis, from thence to Boston, Newport and Worcester,—after having endured, with loss of health, more than two months' confinement in a noisome jail, and suffered the irreparable loss of the confidence and affection of his fellow creatures, after all this, can any man in his senses suppose that he will repeat those actions which have exposed him to such accumulated misfortunes; or that it is not sufficient to warn and deter the most undaunted and hardy from similar practices. If then, the ends of his confinement can be answered, is there, can there be any possible objections to an enlargement? Gentlemen, suppose the worst, suppose he left Worcester with an evil intent, that he joined the enemy in opposition to the country, is it impossible to repent? Is there no indulgence to a returning penitent? Did the returning prodigal receive forgiveness, banquets, the robes and the ring? And shall an unfortunate adventurer receive nothing but severities, chains and rigorous imprisonment? Is not the language of his return the voice of repentence? Is there no allowance to be made for the inexperience of years, and the frailties and imperfections of short-sighted mortals? Your petitioner asks for nothing out of your power to grant, consistent with the general good; for nothing but what is supported by reason and warranted by precedents. Out of the many examples adducible in point, he will produce two that may serve as a lead in the present case: the one of an early, the other of a recent date. In the course of the last winter, you all remember the association of a number of persons at Marshfield and the bordering towns. The address to the then General for troops, fire arms and ammunition in opposition to the country, and the most ardent entreaties of the people. The troops were sent, they received the arms and ammunition, banded with the regulars in hostile array, bade defiance to the authority of the people, and pledged themselves for the support of ministerial measures. After the Lexington battle, they escaped with their mercenary companions to the camp of your enemy. About a fortnight after, a part of those were seen off the coast of Marshfield, were taken, carried to headquarters, examined, and confined only to the limits of particular towns, unless giving bonds for their future good behavior. The other instance is one Jones, from the Eastward, who in the face of a resolution of Congress declaring all persons aiding, assisting, or any way supplying the King's troops, enemies to the people and traitors to the country, was detected in supplying by vessel loads, the ministerial army with lumber, provisions and other necessaries. He was committed to jail, and upon applying, no longer ago than the last session of court, to the Honorable Council by whom he was examined and committed, and who were privy to the charges against him, he was admitted to bail. Shall those taken in arms against the public, and in supplying their avowed enemies, be permitted enlargement, and shall one who has done neither, be consigned over to lingering destruction? Are the accusations against your petitioner, allowing they were all true, more atrocious than the above crimes? Whence, then, the discrimination? Will a town deny to its own inhabitant, what the Generals of the army, and the Council of the Province, granted to greater offenders?

Gentlemen and fellow townsmen, considering you have such precedents to follow, such authority to plead; considering you have ample security tendered, and the safety of society, the ends of confinement and even of punishment will all be answered; considering no rank or elevation in life, no uprightness of heart, no prudence or circumspection of conduct can give infallible security against dungeons and jails; considering the infirmities of the best among us, the vices and ungovernable passions of others, the instability of all human affairs, the numberless unforeseen events that the compass of a year or a day may bring forth, which will teach us candor and forbearance; considering the benignity of the English law, how tenderly it regards the liberty of the subject, how compassionately it accomodates itself to the frailties and imperfections of humanity, how upon these principles it sometimes excuses, and sometimes mitigates the greatest of crimes; when he considers the great charter of freedom, that glorious institution in defence of which many of his countrymen are hazarding their fortunes and jeoparding their lives, breathes nothing but liberty; when he considers his application is to the professed disciples of Him, who by his benevolent precepts cultivates humanity and forgiveness, how when figuring to his followers the tremendous transaction at the tribunal of heaven, He made kindness to prisoners an express condition upon which they were to enter into the glories of His Father; when he considers all these things, he is ready to hope that you will easily adopt a measure, that must prove happy to yourselves, useful to the community, and necessary for your petitioner, in granting him enlargement from a place where he is losing his health and contracting diseases that may either snatch him away in the vigor of years or cause him to drag out a miserable existence in unalleviated pain, misery and distress; your petitioner, as in duty bound, will ever pray.

WORCESTER JAIL, Nov. 21, 1775.

The prayer of the petitioner was granted, and on the

5th of December, after a confinement of 76 days, he was removed to his mother's house, and on the 15th of December he received permission from the Council to reside in Lancaster, being required to furnish bonds, to be filed with the Colony Treasurer, in the sum of £1000, that he would not go out of the limits of that town.

In January, 1776, Samuel Curtis and William Young, were elected as magistrates to exercise the powers of justices of the peace, for the preservation of good order.

In May, Nathan Baldwin was chosen to take acknowledgments of debts, where the amount exceeded twenty pounds.

The town was called upon for blankets for the army, and twenty-seven were immediately furnished.

Men were wanted to reinforce the army around Boston, and thirty-two were levied and forwarded from Worcester.

At a town meeting held on the 23rd of May, a motion was made and seconded to see if the town would support Independence, if Congress should declare the American Colonies independent of Great Britain, and it was voted "*that we will sustain the measure with our lives and fortunes*, and that the town clerk serve Mr. Joshua Bigelow, Representative for this town, with a copy of the vote for his instruction."

In June, 56 men were required as the quota of the town, toward the formation of battalions, destined to cooperate with the Continental troops in New York and Canada.

On the 26th of June, the County Convention of Committees of Correspondence resolved, that as the Congress had established a price for Bohea Tea and other articles. any one who should charge a higher price than that established should be considered an enemy to the American cause and treated as such, and called on all Committees of Inspection and people generally to be vigilant in detecting such persons.

In July, men were furnished to support the army in the Northern Department.

CHAPTER V.

Declaration of Independence—Subsequent celebration of the event—Calls for more troops promptly met—New York sends its tories to Worcester jail—Address of Committee of Correspondence recommending milder measures concerning suspected persons—One seventh male inhabitants drafted—Escape and capture of a portion of the New York captives—Town excited because of change of basis of Representation to General Court—Bounty voted to recruits—Money raised by general tax—Tories prosecuted—Soldiers march to the relief of the Northern army—Another draft—A company march to oppose Burgoyne—Burgoyne's captive army pass through town—Town voted to approve of Confederation of States—Town voted not to approve Constitution recommended for State—Banishment and confiscation of the property of certain tories.

The events of the beginning of the year 1776 hastened the action of the Colonies, by which they formally severed themselves from all political connection with Great Britain. On the 4th of July, the celebrated Declaration of Independence was adopted by the Provincial Congress, assembled at Philadelphia. It rehearses in concise and unmistakable language the various tyrannical acts of the mother country, and the reasons growing out of them, why the Colonies should be Free and Independent States. It was immediately read at the head of the army, and transmitted as speedily as possible to the authorities to whom the people had confided their civil interests in the various sections of the country.

On Sunday, the 14th of July, a copy of this document on its way to Boston, was intercepted, and read from the porch of the Old South meeting-house by Mr. Isaiah Thomas, and thus, for the first time on Massachusetts soil, that instrument, the key note of which is, "that all men are born free and equal," and which declared the American Colonies to be Free and Independent States, was read, and liberty proclaimed.

Monday, the 22nd, was set apart for the purpose of celebrating the event, and the following account of the proceedings is from the Spy of July 24, 1776.

"On Monday last, a number of patriotic gentlemen of this town, animated with a love of their country, and to show their approbation of the measures lately taken by the Grand Council of America, assembled on the green near the liberty pole, where, after having displayed the colors of the thirteen Confederate Colonies of America, the bells were set ringing and the drums a beating; after which the declaration of Independence of the United States was read to a large and respectable body, among whom were the Selectmen and Committee of Correspondence assembled on the occasion, who testified their approbation by repeated huzzas, firing of musketry and cannon, bonfires and other demonstrations of joy. When the arms of that tyrant in Britain, George the III, of execrable memory, which in former times decorated, but of late disgraced the court house in this town, were committed to the flames and consumed to ashes: after which a select company of the sons of freedom, repaired to the tavern lately known by the Sign of the King's Arms, which odious signature of despotism, was taken down by order of the people, which was cheerfully complied with by the innkeeper, where the following toasts were drank, and the evening spent with joy on the commencement of the happy era.

1. Prosperity and perpetuity to the United States of America. 2. The president of the Grand Council of America. 3. The Grand Council of America. 4. His excellency Gen. Washington. 5. All the Generals in the American Army. 6. Commodore Hopkins. 7. The officers and soldiers of the American Army. 8. The officers and seamen in the America navy. 9. The patriots of America. 10. Every friend of America. 11. George rejected and liberty protected. 12. Success to the American arms. 13. Sore eyes to all tories and a chestnut burr for an eye stone. 14. Perpetual itching without the benefit of scratching to the enemies of America. 15. The Council and Representatives of the State of Massachusetts Bay. 16. The officers and soldiers in the Massachusetts service. 17. The memory of the brave Gen. Warren. 18. The memory of the magnanimous Gen. Montgomery. 19. Speedy redemption to all the officers and soldiers who are now prisoners of war among our enemies. 20. The State of Massachusetts Bay. 21. The town of Boston. 22. The Selectmen and Committee of Correspondence for the town of Worcester. 23. May the enemies of America be laid at her feet.

24. May the freedom and independency of America endure till the sun grows dim with age and this earth returns to chaos.

The greatest decency and good order was observed, and at a suitable time each man returned to his respective home.

On the 14th of July,* the county convention of Committees of Correspondence called upon the Committees of the several towns to transmit forthwith to the Standing Committee, the names of such persons in their respective towns, as were esteemed to be notoriously inimical to the rights of America.

At a meeting held in September, the question was submitted whether the town would give its voice toward empowering the Council and House of Representatives to adopt such a constitution and frame of government as was most conducive to the safety, peace and happiness of the State. It was determined that, considering so many of the inhabitants were absent in the army, it was inexpedient to act in the matter.

On the 10th of this month one-fifth part of the militia were ordered to New York; one-fourth part of the remainder were required to be in readiness to march at a moment's notice. Troops were needed for the defence of Boston and other places on the coast. Worcester met all these calls promptly.

The roll of Capt. William Gates' Company, in Col. Jonathan Holman's regiment in Chelsea camp, New York, Sept. 4, 1776, gives the names of fifty-four† men from Worcester.

Volunteers from this town marched to the relief of Rhode Island, and remained during a portion of the winter.

---

* Doubtless an error, the 14th fell on Sunday. Lincoln gives the above date.

† Lincoln states the number to be 35. The original roll in possession of the American Antiquarian Society, gives 54 as the number.

In Col. Craft's regiment of artillery, were twenty-four men from Worcester.

In October, 1776, a committee of the convention of the State of New York, appointed for inquiring into, detecting and defeating all conspiracies which might be formed in said State against the liberties of America, sent to the care of the Committee of Correspondence of Worcester, thirty-one prisoners charged with treasonable practices, who were committed to the jail.

The Committee of Correspondence for the town, issued the following in November.

[From the Massachusetts Spy, Nov. 27, 1776.]

In Committee Chamber, Worcester, Nov. 18, 1776.

As expedients are no longer wise, prudent and politic, than the reasons on which they were founded exist, and effects are reversed by a mutation of causes; as the demands of our country are continually variating, and the complexion of public affairs incessantly altering; as our dangers and our fears subside by the approach of the enemy, and their acts of division have produced unanimity; as the Resolve of the State on the 8th of May, 1775, was a temporary provision, and has had its operation; as the resolution of our predecessors in office, disarming and confining to this town a number of its inhabitants, was expressly to prevent their joining our avowed enemies, and to deprive them of the means of obstructing measures adopted for the common defence; as the suffering, servile, spurned attendance on a passing camp, the fate of the parricides who have joined the adversary, must deter all, but the mad, from repeating the experiment, and the recent epistolary lamentations of disappointed refugees extorts the Poet's cry:

> Ye Gods! if there be a man I hate,
> Let attendance and dependence be his fate.

As this day's spectacle* of wretched, deluded objects, the ruined, exiled grovellings, spated out of a sister State, is a serious warning to persons sporting with the feelings of a whole continent, be they whom, where, or what they may, and the Worcester gaol filled with the same engaging geniuses, will remain a standing memento of future dangers to the

---

*This day, about one hundred tories passed through this town under a military guard, on their way to Exeter.

unfriendly; as the Congress for the Continent have supposed, there were some who through weakness deceived others, from an apprehension that British power was irresistable, frightening them into opposition, and recommended such as subjects of kindness, reason and reformation; as the privilege of repenting is one of the most precious indulgences incident to erring mortals, and when attended with an amendment of principle and practice, is happy for the man, useful to society and pleasing to heaven; as some of the suspected are loud in proclaiming their affection for their country, their grievances from a disarmed confinement and their readiness for exertion in the general struggle; as early in the dispute, when the expediency of measures was the topic of the day *possibly* a mere difference of opinion was the too slender ground of some hasty suspicions, and a subsequent change of sentiment and conduct may have laid the foundations for forgiveness and friendship, which are equally Christian and political duties: as an army potent enough to make all Europe tremble, and a fleet sufficiently fiery to have set the seas on flames, have been able in a summer's campaign, only to effect the possession of lines deserted from policy, a few evacuated towns, the retreat of a picket guard, and the rout of an advanced detachment, or a rambling party, by the weight of solid columns and heavy artillery, the timorous and the doubting must have become courageous and resolved; as the disaffected from principle, have not now to learn from the enemy's not attacking our main army or effecting a progress into the country, from their hugging the borders of the ocean under cover of their hostile arks, that the conquest of America is an event never to be expected; as under such circumstances, joining the regulars would be a perpetual exile, poverty, slavery and death: and coöperating with freemen, with Americans, would be rational, manly, triumph, freedom and glory; as the present struggle is bottomed on such principles as ought to make every man a party, and the time is hastening when there can be no neuter, no drones in the hive; as the restraining an Englishman to a single town is in derogation of a common right, depriving him of his arms, an infraction on liberty, and recording him a tory, stamping him with infamy, and cannot be justified, but upon principles of public necessity; as the preparation for war is a duty enforced by the law of our being, and the weapons of death are necessary for the preservation of our own and the lives of our neighbors; that the deceiver and the deceived, the timorous and the obstinate, the dissembler and the undesigning, the abusive and the well meaning, the ambiguous and the honest, may all have a full, fair, and ample opportunity of giving full, fair, and ample assurance of their friendship to Independence, and their readiness to assist and join their countrymen in opposition to both open and secret enemies; that the discontented may be disarmed of every objection, that every barrier to their duty may be removed, and suitable encouragement tendered, and finally, as a more effectual provision is made and now making, both for the restraint and punishment of him who *dares* to be a dangerous man and makes war upon the rights and interests of rising States, either by avowed exertions, or concealed machinations, and as no good reason can be given for continuing the mere existence of the Resolve made by our predecessors aforesaid:

Therefore, Resolved, that it is inexpedient that the Resolution of the late Committee of this town, disarming and confining a number of its inhabitants be any longer in force; that such persons once more be put on a standing with the rest of their fellow countrymen, that they be allowed the privileges of Englishmen, of friends to their country, of passing where and when they please, until they evidence by their conduct and behavior a different character, and that such as have arms in the possession of the Committee may receive the same by making application to Mr. Baldwin, their chairman.

2ndly. Resolved, that it be recommended to all the firm and tried friends to their country, to endeavor and convince persons of every degree, character and complexion, that the cause we are engaged in is of too much dignity to be sullied by rashness, too important, too seriously important, to be weakened by tumult, divisions and party strife; that liberty receives strength and vigor from prudence and consideration: that justice, equity and regularity, and in some instances moderation, are her dearest friends; that she courts virtue as her bosom companion, and shuns vice as her dangerous enemy; and therefore equally avoiding feverish fits of political heat, and [   ] banishing from their breasts all personal prejudices, private piques, narrow opinions, illiberal distinctions and unbecoming jealousies; displaying a magnanimity proportioned to the importance and danger of the struggle, cultivating harmony of sentiment, and unanimity of councils, and carefully distinguishing between the friend and the foe; that it is wisdom (acting discreetly, firmly, unitedly and spiritedly) to receive all such to their favor, friendship and confidence, who will give ample and satisfactory assurances of their readiness to join in the defence of their much injured country, and their steady, persevering attachment to her glorious cause, at the same time to exercise a vigilant attention to those who continue notoriously in opposition; those who secretly influence under the principle of an affected neutrality, and those who labor to conceal themselves under a despicable cloak of cunning duplicity, if any such there be.

3rdly. Resolved, that it be recommended to the good people of this town, that they use their utmost endeavor immediately to equip themselves with every implement of war, as the necessary means of defence from a foreign attack, or internal insurrection.

Per Order of the Committee of Correspondence, Inspection and Safety of Worcester.

NATHAN BALDWIN, Chairman.

Early in January, 1777, a requisition was made on the town for 32 blankets, followed on the 26th by a draft of every seventh of the male inhabitants over 16 years of age, to complete the quota of Massachusetts in the Continental army, to serve eight months at least.

On the 12th of January, 12 persons sent from the State of New York, and confined here for treasonable practices against the Colonies, broke out of the jail by the assistance of some tories, but were apprehended and brought back to prison.

An Act of the General Court changing the ratio of representation, excited a great deal of opposition from the interior of State. The town of Sutton recommended a county convention to draw up a remonstrance, and to petition for its repeal. The Committees of Correspondence for the several towns in the county, in convention, passed resolutions to the same effect. At a meeting of the inhabitants of Worcester on the 18th of March, a committee, consisting of Levi Lincoln, Nathan Baldwin, and Samuel Curtis, reported instructions to be given to the Representative to the General Court as follows:

"Worcester, March 11, 1777. At a town meeting legally warned, a committee was appointed to prepare instructions to be given to the Representative for the town of Worcester, respecting a late law made and passed in the General Court, entitled, 'An act for the more equal representation of the inhabitants of this State.'

The committee beg leave to report as follows.

First: Resolved, that in the opinion of this town the said act for enlarging the representation aforesaid, was impolitic, unnecessary, unconstitutional and attended with many consequences grievous to the good people of the inland parts of the State.

Second: Resolved, that it be recommended to Joshua Bigelow, Esq., and he is hereby requested and desired to use his utmost endeavor, at the General Court of this State, to obtain a repeal of the said act before writs are issued for a new choice of Representatives.

Resolved, that the town clerk furnish Joshua Bigelow, Esq., with a copy of these resolves as soon as may be."

The report was accepted by a unanimous vote.

In February, a requisition being made upon each town in the State, for shirts, stockings and other clothing for the Massachusetts troops in the Continental army, Worcester supplied sixty-two sets.

On the 18th of March, a bounty of £20 was voted in addition to the grants of the State and Continent, to soldiers enlisting to fill the quota of the town.

April 7th. It was voted, "that the sum of £1656 2s. 3d. 2f. be and hereby is granted, and that the said sum be assessed upon the polls and estates of the inhabitants of this town, in order to defray the expenses of the present war with Great Britain, from the commencement thereof to the present time, including the expense of hiring our present quota of men for filling up the battallions of the Continental army, and that each person be allowed for all such public service as he or they may have done in the said war since the commencement thereof."

On the 19th of May, Capt. Ebenezer Lovell, David Bigelow, Dr. John Green, and Ezekiel Howe, were chosen Representatives to the General Court.

On the 16th of June, £1247 were granted to pay

bounty to such soldiers as have enlisted and shall enlist for three years or during the war.

In the warrant for a town meeting to be held on the 16th of June, an article was inserted as follows:

> 4th. For the town to act on a late Act of the General Assembly of the State, entitled, "An act for securing this and the other of the United States against the dangers to which they are exposed, by the internal enemies thereof, and for the town to do and act thereon any thing that they may think proper."

In accordance with this article, the Selectmen presented a list of the names of a number of persons whom they esteemed as enemies, and dangerous to this and the other United States of America, and a number of others were nominated at the meeting, and the nominations being seconded, by vote of the town their names were added to the lists, agreeable to the late Act of the General Assembly. The list of names is as follows, viz: Nahum Willard, David Moore, Samuel Moore, Cornelius Stowell, Jacob Chamberlain, John Curtis, Gardner Chandler, Micah Johnson, Joshua Johnson, William Curtis, Nathan Patch, Joseph Blair, John Barnard, Palmer Goulding, Jacob Stevens, Joseph Clark, and James Hart, Jr. The town made choice of Mr. William Dawes to collect the evidence against these persons, agreeable to the Act. At an adjourned meeting held on the 30th, the names of Robert Crawford and Micah Johnson, Jr., were added to this list of internal enemies. Doubts having arisen as to the justice of this method of convicting persons without a trial, or opportunity for defence, the town clerk was directed to suspend making a return of the names of these persons, excepting Nahum Willard, David Moore, Samuel Moore, John Curtis, William Curtis, Micah Johnson, Jr., and Robert Crawford. At a meeting held in December, it was "voted to receive

Capt. John Curtis, Nahum Willard, David Moore, Samuel Moore, and Micah Johnson, Jr., into the town's favor, and that further prosecution against them as enemies to the United States of America shall cease, they paying the costs that have arisen already by means of their being prosecuted as enemies to the said United States, agreeable to their petition."

A company of men in which were some from this town, left here in July, to march to the assistance of the army in Northern New York. They were commanded by Jesse Stone of the South Parish, with Nathaniel Harrington of Worcester, as First Lieutenant. Leaving Worcester, they marched through Leicester, Spencer, Brookfield, Ware, Belchertown, Amherst, Hadley, Northampton, Chesterfield, Worthington, Lanesboro, Williamstown, over Hoosac Mountain through Pownal to Bennington, the march occupying a week. On their arrival they were joined to Col. Job Cushing's regiment and continued towards Ticonderoga. They soon received orders to return and reinforce Gen. Stark without delay, and arrived at Bennington on Sunday, the day after the battle, and performed the duty of guarding the British prisoners. The regiment remained until about the 29th of August, when they were dismissed. The company returned to Worcester through New Marlboro, Coleraine, Guilford, Hinsdale, Warwick, Orange, Athol, Petersham, Barre, Rutland, and Paxton, arriving home Sept. 2nd, having been absent within two days of two months.

In August every sixth man was drafted for the Northern army for three months.

The successes of Burgoyne caused much alarm, and by desire of Brig. Gen. Warner, a company numbering 73 men, under Lieut. Col. Benjamin Flagg, with David Chadwick as Captain, marched as far as Hadley, on their way to Albany. The alarm having subsided and the danger being over they returned home.

Early in October, General Burgoyne and his captured army passed through town on their way to their imprisonment near Boston.

On the 10th of November, £160 was granted for eight soldiers to fill the quota of the town.

An Act of the General Court, providing for the payment of interest on the State debt, and restraining the circulation of bills of less denomination than £10, caused much opposition. A convention was held in November, and petitioned the Legislature to repeal the Act.

In December, a committtee, consisting of William Dawes, Samuel Brown, and Asa Ward, was chosen to provide for the families of soldiers.

On the 12th of January, 1778, it was voted unanimously that the Confederation agreed upon by the United States in General Congress assembled, was agreeable to the minds of the people of this town.

In February, 1778, thirty-seven men from Capt. Ebenezer Lovell's company, and twenty-six from Capt. Joshua Whitney's company, enlisted for three years.

A requisition for clothing was made in March, and Worcester furnished 62 sets of shirts, shoes and stockings for the army.

A battalion being formed for service on the Hudson River, Worcester furnished 15 men. Twelve men were drafted for the Continental army, to serve nine months.

A town meeting was held April 13th, for the purpose of ascertaining whether the inhabitants approved or disapproved of the Constitution or form of Government agreed on by a convention of the State. At an adjourned meeting held May 19th, upon the question being put, there were nine votes in favor of the Constitution, and forty-nine against it. At this meeting Samuel Curtis was elected Representive to the General Court.

Six men were drafted in June, to join an expedition to Rhode Island and four to guard prisoners from Burgoyne's army.

On the 18th of November, £660, 12s. 10d. were granted to pay Wm. Young, Esq., Josiah Pierce, Nathan Perry, and John Kelso, for money borrowed by them to pay soldiers enlisted for the town in the Continental army.

The General Assembly passed an Act forbidding the return of the leading tories who had left the State and joined the enemy, and notifying them that if they were found a second time within the limits of the state, after the passage of the Act, they should suffer death therefor. The list of persons thus banished, includes the following, who formerly resided in Worcester, viz: John Chandler, Rufus Chandler, William Chandler, James Putnam, Adam Walker, William Paine. The latter was allowed to return to Worcester in 1793, where he resided until his death in 1833.

In March, 1779, £2,000 were levied and assessed for the support of the war, and the officers of the militia were directed to fill the quota of the town for the continental army by enlistment or draft.

In April, three teams were required and furnished for the transportation of warlike stores to Springfield.

On the 13th of April, the General Court passed an Act to confiscate the estates of certain notorious conspirators against the Government and Liberties of the inhabitants of the State of Massachusetts Bay, and recited that the persons therein named, had justly incurred the forfeiture of all their properties, rights and liberties held under and derived from the Government Laws of the State, and should be considered as aliens, and that all their goods and chattels, lands and tenements should escheat and inure to the use of the Government and people of the State. Afterwards, in the same year, a Resolve was passed, directing the sale of the confiscated estates at public auction, and a committee was appointed for the purpose of carrying the Resolve into effect. In accordance with this Act and Resolve, the property of the Chandlers, Col. Putnam and others was confiscated for the benefit of the government of the State.

In June, 10 soldiers were raised for the army, and 62 sets of clothing furnished.

A contribution was taken in church, for the relief of the people of Newport, suffering from the devastations of the British, and £78 were collected.

The Town obtained by loan £5,200 for the payment of bounties.

CHAPTER VI.

Convention to consider the question of Finance—Action of the town thereon—County Convention for the same purpose and its proceedings, fixing prices of labor and produce—Delegates elected to a Constitutional Convention—Further requisitions for men and means answered—Bill of Rights and Constitution accepted, with some exceptions—First election under the Constitution—More men and provisions supplied for the army—Worcester thinks she has contributed more money and men than her proportion—Surrender of Cornwallis—Jubilation—Instructions to Representative on grievances.

A Convention of delegates from all parts of the State assembled at Concord on the 14th of July, to adopt measures to relieve the people from the disastrous effects of the great depreciation of the currency, and the high prices of the necessaries of life. The delegates from Worcester were Joseph Barber and David Bigelow. Prices for the leading articles of produce and merchandise were established, and recommendations to the Committees of Correspondence for the several towns were adopted.

A town meeting was held here August 2d, and the doings and resolves of the Concord Convention were highly approved, and a committee was chosen to join with the Committee of Correspondence in carrying out the spirit and intent of its proceedings and resolutions. A committee was also chosen, consisting of Messrs. William Stearns, Nathan Baldwin and Joseph Allen, to consider and report such resolutions as they deemed proper to be passed and entered into by the town relative to the appreciation of the currency, and to lay the same before the town at an adjourned meeting. At this adjourned meeting, held August 5th, they reported the following resolutions, which were accepted and adopted :

"Whereas, the reinstating and supporting the credit of our paper currency is of the highest importance, in respect to the political salvation of the United States of America,—and as it is the duty of all distinct bodies in the Commonwealth, as well corporate as individual, to exert their utmost efforts to carry into effect a purpose of such indispensible necessity,

Therefore, we, the inhabitants of the town of Worcester, in town meeting assembled, do resolve,

1st. That unanimity and fortitude in carrying into effectual execution the measures so judiciously recommended and urged by the late Convention held at Concord, will be a specific remedy and antidote against the depreciation of our currency, render it of value, and give it a permanent establishment.

2d. Resolved, that the harmony, unanimity and perfect coalescence of the different interests in the late Convention are a shining example, worthy of the imitation of this and our sister States, and a happy presage of the effectual completion of the design in contemplation.

3d. Resolved, that as our public affairs were in a great degree reduced to the alarming state they were in, and the good people of these States involved in the greatest danger by men destitute of all principles except those of avarice and circumvention,

Therefore, it is our duty to exhibit those who shall continue in the same line of behavior in the future, to the view of the public, that they may be subjected to the frowns of the community and branded with infamy.

4th. As many of the respectable merchants and fair traders have retired from business, their places have been supplied by an augmented number of locusts and canker worms in human form, who have increased and proceeded along the road to plunder, until they have become odiously formidable, and their contagious influence dangerously prevalent,

Therefore, Resolved, that such persons ought not to be admitted to bear a part in any mercantile consultations, but should be considered pestilential mushrooms of trade which have come up in the night of public calamity, and ought to perish in the same night.

5th. Whereas, regrators in the public market, forestallers, engrossers of the produce of the country, and higglers, have had a great share in depreciating the public currency by their pernicious practices,

Resolved, that all such persons are guilty of a dangerous opposition to the measures necessary to promote the well-being and prosperity of this country, and ought to be subjected to the resentment and indignation of the public, whether their conduct proceeds from a general disaffection to public measures, and the Independence of these States, or from private motives of sordid avarice.

6th. And as there is another set of persons equally atrocious, and dangerous offenders against the safety of the country, viz: those who withhold corn, and other necessaries of life,

Resolved, that whoever refuses to sell the surplus of the produce of his farm, and retains the same to procure a higher price, by means of an artificial scarcity, is very criminally accessory to the calamities of the country, and ought to be subjected to those penalties and disabilities which are due to an inveterate enemy.

7th. Resolved, that we shall consider any fraudulent subterfuge, or artful evasion of the rules and arrangements that shall be made here in conformity to the measures recommended by the Convention, as equally criminal with a direct violation of the express letter of such rules and regulations.

8th. And whereas, this town has chosen a large Committee of Inspection to join with, aid and assist the Committee of Correspondence in carrying into execution such rules and regulations as shall be made here, agreeable to the proceedings and resolutions of said Convention, we do resolve to support said Committee in the full and complete discharge of their duty in this behalf, so long as such measures shall be deemed necessary by the public.

9th. Resolved, that this town will elect delegates to meet in another Convention at Concord, at the time and for the purpose by the late Convention recommended.

10th. Resolved, that as this town is fully sensible of the necessity of the different interests harmonizing and acting in full concert with each other for the accomplishment of the happy purposes aforementioned, we will exert ourselves to the utmost of our power, to cement that union which so happily subsists between the fair and upright merchant and the honest yeomanry of the State."

A County Convention composed of delegates from the several towns was held August 31st, 1779, for the purpose of carrying into effect the measures recommended by Congress to the inhabitants of the United States, and by the Convention at Concord to the people of this State. Thirty-eight towns were represented. An account of their proceedings follows.

"The delegates from a large majority of the towns within the county of Worcester, in consequence of the late resolves, address, &c. of a State Convention held at Concord on the 14th ult., to manifest our hearty acquiescence in their wise and salutary measures there agreed upon, and as firm friends to the sacred and important cause of our distressed country, to use our most vigorous efforts for removing as far as in us lies that cloud of impending ruin, which at present hovers over our country by means of the amazing depreciation of our currency, and the exorbitant prices of the necessaries of life; having carefully and deliberately considered those important matters, have determined upon the following resolutions, which they conceive must have a tendency to answer the desired end, and hope they will appear to every friend of his country to be calculated for securing the political salvation thereof.

1. Resolved unanimously (as our opinion) that from and after the publication of the proceedings of this Convention, the following enumerated articles of merchandise and country produce be not sold within this county at a higher price than is hereafter affixed to them, nor any laborer or mechanic take a higher price for his or her service than is here specified, viz: Indian Corn, £3 12s. per bushel; Rye, £5 2s. per bushel; Wheat, £8 2s.; Oats, £1 16s.; Beef, 5s. 6d. per lb., until the 1st of September next, and 4s. 6d. afterwards; Lamb, Mutton and Veal, 3s. 6d.; Butter, 11s.; Cheese, 5s. 6d.; Vegetables in proportion; Cider, £4 per barrel; Hay, £1 10s. per cwt.; Sheep's wool, £1 4s. per lb., in the fleece of the best quality; Flax, 12s.; Laborers in Husbandry £2 14s. per day, in the best part of the season, and at other times in the usual proportion; Women's labor £2 per week, weaving 5s. per yd. wide tow cloth, and all other weaving in the usual proportion; Teamsters, £1 per mile for carrying a ton gross weight and loaded, one way; Horse keeping 15s. per night by hay, 8s. by grass; Keeping a yoke of oxen, £1 per night by hay, and 10s. by grass; Good common dinner, 13s. and all other victualling in the usual proportion; Lodging 3s. per night; West India Flip, 15s. per mug; West India Toddy, 15s. per bowl; New England Flip or Toddy, 12s. per mug or bowl; Cider, 3s. per mug; All other liquors in small

quantities in the usual proportion; Green Hides, 4s. per lb.; Sole Leather £1 per lb.; Men's best shoes, £6 per pair; Shoeing horses £4 all round with steel at toe and heel; A narrow axe of the best quality £6; Best Salt £12 per bushel, fifty miles from market; West India rum, £6 per gall; New England rum, £5 2s.; Good Yarn Stockings, £3 12s. per pair. The labor of mechanics to be in the usual proportion to the labor of farmers."

Resolutions were passed recommending to the inhabitants of each town in the county to fix the prices of the more minute articles of labor, produce, &c., and also recommending each town to choose a large Committee to see that these Resolves were effectually carried into execution, and to deal with every person who should be guilty of a breach of these Resolutions, as an enemy to this country. The utmost unanimity and cordiality marked all the proceedings of the Convention. Levi Lincoln, Joseph Allen, and David Bigelow were chosen delegates to a Convention for framing a Constitution.

On the 16th of August, £892, 16s. were granted to pay for the shirts, shoes and stockings to be procured for the soldiers.

September 14th, a requisition was made for 31 blankets. Eight soldiers were raised September 21st, for the Rhode Island service at an expense of £610. Thirteen men were sent to join Gen. Washington on the Hudson River, and £2,515 were granted to reimburse the Committee for money paid out for hire, bounty and mileage.

In May, 1780, the town furnished 43 sets of blankets, shirts and stockings.

On the 22d of May, Samuel Curtis was chosen Representative to the General Court.

On the 29th, £290 were granted to procure men to do duty at Rutland, and £750 for the hire of soldiers.

The Bill of Rights and Frame of Government was submitted to the people of the town, and after having been read paragraph by paragraph, it was " voted to accept thereof, except the 3d and 20th articles in the Bill of Rights, the 4th article of the 1st section in chapter 1st of the Constitution, the 1st article of the 3d section in the same chapter, the 9th article of the same, the 7th article of the 1st section of the 2d chapter, and the 3d and 7th articles of chapter 6th, which the town disapprove of in their present form."

In June, 22 men were furnished for six months' service. In July, 28 men were raised for three months, and five men for duty at Springfield; twelve horses were provided for transportation and cavalry service.

£30,000 were granted July 20th, for the purpose of paying the six and three months' men their advance money.

The first election under the new Constitution took place in September, and in this town, resulted in a vote of 55 for John Hancock for Governor, and 20 for James Bowdoin.

The town being required to furnish her quota of 17,640 pounds of beef for the army, an assessment of £529 4s. was voted, October 23d. £92 11s. 3d. additional were granted in November. On the 2d of December a requisition being made for 29 men for the army, and great difficulty being experienced in obtaining them, the citizens were divided into 29 classes, according to the amount of taxes paid, and each class was required to furnish one man. Any who should refuse to contribute their share towards the amount required, were to be reported to the assessors, and the sums due, were included in the next general tax. By this means the men were procured.

£1270 3s. 3d. were granted January 21st, 1781, for the town's quota of beef, and on Feb. 9th, £339 9s. 9d. to discharge contracts made with the 6 and 3 months' men. June 22nd, a requisition was made for blankets, and 59 sets of articles of clothing. July 9th, £400 in gold or silver were voted for the purchase of beef in accordance with a requisition of June 22th. On the 23rd, £414 in hard money were granted for the purpose of raising soldiers. Aug. 6th, £197 10s. in gold were voted for the purpose of paying for the horses that the Selectmen had procured the year before, according to a resolution of the General Court. On the 13th, £116 5s. 4d. in gold were voted for the purchase of the town's quota of clothing.

The people of Worcester feeling that they had been called upon for more than their just proportion of money and men in support of the war, instructed Samuel Curtis, Esq., Representative, on the 30th of August, to lay the following petition before the General Court.

"To the Honorable, the Senate and House of Representatives of the Commonwealth of Massachusetts, in General Court assembled.

The Petition of the Inhabitants of the Town of Worcester, humbly sheweth :—That for several years last past, your petitioners have been called upon by Government, for larger sums of money, and greater numbers of soldiers than their just proportion, which they can make evidently to appear if your Honors would indulge them with an opportunity therefor. Your petitioners have heretofore applied to your Honors for relief, but are informed that their omission in not returning a valuation in the year 1778, bars them from a possibility of redress; a circumstance so unfortunate to your petitioners as compels them, as well to vindicate themselves from any supposed contumacy towards Government as to open a way to their relief, to state that matter in its just light. The town knew nothing of the omission of the assessors with respect to the valuation before mentioned, until a disproportionate assessment led them to inquire the cause: your petitioners afterwards called upon the assessors whose duty it was to have returned the valuation, to declare their motives for the supposed neglect, and were by them informed that the orders for taking a new valuation did not reach them in season; your petitioners would beg leave to observe, that admitting the assessors were culpable, as it was without the consent or even knowledge of the town, yet in their apprehension they have a full claim to be considered and relieved in the premises. Your petitioners, therefore, again most earnestly pray your Honors to take their case into your wise consideration, and as they wish not to elude the burthen of the day, that a full inquiry may be made as to the justice of their complaint, and that they may experience that equity which they apprehend their case entitles them to, both with respect to future taxes and those that have been made since the last general valuation, and as in duty bound, your petitioners shall ever pray."

The surrender of Cornwallis at Yorktown, having taken place on the 19th of October, 1781, the Massachusetts Spy of Nov. 8th, announced the event in language at once extravagant and expressive.

"On Friday evening arrived in this town a further confirmation, with some of the articles of capitulation (as published under the Hartford head) of the surrender of Lieut. General *Earl Cornwallis* and his *Whole Army*, composed of the flower of the British troops in America, to the allied army, commanded by our illustrious General Washington, and the fleet of his Most Christian Majesty, commanded by Count de Grasse; an event that must affect every patriotic American with joy and pleasing sensibility. In consequence of this glorious intelligence, yesterday morning was ushered in by ringing of bells, discharging of cannon, displaying of colors, attended with the shouts of a grateful populace, and even Aurora advanced and unlocked the ruddy gates of the morning, with a sympathetic smile. At noon a number of gentlemen assembled and dined together at the Sun Tavern, after which the following toasts were drank, with the discharge of cannon. In the evening were illuminations, &c.

1. The Sages of America in Congress assembled.
2. America's Royal friend, his Most Christian Majesty.
3. The Saviour of his Country, General Washington.
4. The Illustrious Count de Grasse.
5. The Victorious General Greene, and his band of Heroes.
6. Our Brethren in the field.
7. The Army and Navy of our brave Allies.

8. May every American Soldier be a Hector and his wife a Penelope.*

9. The memory of those Heroes whose blood has nourished our Independence.

10. The friends of America throughout the Globe.

11. May America ever breed a race of Heroes, whose actions will be sounded in the Trump of Fame.

12. May America support her Independence until the ravages of time shall annihilate the World.

13. May meek-eyed Peace, supported by Honor and Glory soon fertilize the deserts of America."

---

* Though we are sensible that Penelope was not the wife of Hector, yet her life and her fortune were more consonant to our wishes than that of Adromache.

The General Court having passed an Act imposing duties on spiritous liquors, teas, &c., the town, through a Committee consisting of Timothy Paine, Esq., Nathan Baldwin and Cornelius Stowell, instructed Samuel Curtis, Esq., Representative, to endeavor to have the Act repealed.

Six men were drafted for the army in March, 1782, this being the last requisition made on this town.

A petition, signed by Ebenezer Lovell, David Moore, Asa Moore, Robert Smith, Joseph Barber, Nathaniel Harrington, Nathaniel Brooks, Ephraim Miller, Moses Miller, and John Mower, was presented to the Selectmen on the 18th of May, praying that a town meeting might be called for the purpose of instructing Mr. Curtis, the Representative, to endeavor to obtain a redress of grievances, which they considered they were laboring under. In accordance with this petition, a meeting was held on the 8th of June, and the following instructions were reported and adopted.

WORCESTER, June 8, 1782.

To SAMUEL CURTIS, ESQ.

" SIR: We, reposing special trust and confidence in your great patriotism, conduct and fidelity, have elected you to represent us in the

Great and General Court the present year; notwithstanding our reliance on your wisdom and integrity, we think it necessary to instruct you relative to some particular matters of grievance, which we think we labor under, viz:

1. That a Receiver General of this extensive Commonwealth should be a Justice of the Pleas in the county of Middlesex, by which he is rendered unable to attend his office as Treasurer of the Commonwealth, during the time he attends the courts in said county, by which many persons have been, and others no doubt, will be put to considerable expense, besides loss of time and disappointment, who have business with him as Treasurer.

2. As there is a recommendation of Congress, that such officers as have been deranged, and not in actual service, have half pay during life, if said recommendation has, or should take place, we look upon it as a great grievance.

3. That the members of the General Court, when acting as committees of the same, have large wages over and above their pay as Representatives, is a grievance, which we justly complain of.

4. That Representatives having nine shillings per day, considering the scarcity of money, and the difficulty of obtaining thereof, being almost double what they formerly had, when money was much plentier and easier to be had, we think a grievance.

5. We think it a great grievance that there has not been general settlement with the Treasurer of this Commonwealth, and with all others who have been entrusted with the expenditure of public monies, and have not accounted for the same.

6. We think it a grievance that the state of the Treasury is not known to the inhabitants of this Commonwealth, and would have you use your influence, that in future, the General Court transmit to every town, annually, an account of the expenditures of all public money.

7. As the sitting of the General Court in the town of Boston, is attended with many inconveniences, we think said Court's sitting in said town a grievance.

8. That the sitting of the Court of Common Pleas, and General Sessions of the Peace, at the same time, much interfere with each other, by which means the county is put to the cost of paying many Justices many days, when much less time would answer the purpose as well.

9. It has been represented that there have been large grants of land made to Alexander Shepard and others, lying in the old Pro-

vince of Maine, that there has not been a more strict enquiry made whether their claims do not far exceed their original grants, is complained of.

These, Sir, are our sentiments as matters of grievance, which we instruct you to use your utmost exertions to guard against, and obtain redress, as becomes an individual member of the General Assembly."

CHAPTER VII.

Slavery abolished by decision of the Court at Worcester—Treaty of Peace—Celebration—The question of absentees and refugees considered.

The subject of slavery had for a long term of years caused much uneasiness among the people. The hearts and minds of patriots and philanthropists had been quickened to a sense of the atrocious wickedness of man holding property in man, and the public conscience was gradually becoming susceptible to appeals for its abolition.

The traffic was never sanctioned in this Province, and under the Colonial and Provincial Charters the slave trade was deprecated as a disgrace to humanity. The holding of slaves was not general, being confined to the wealthier classes.

In 1767, Joshua Bigelow, Representative to the General Court, had been instructed to use his influence to "obtain a law to put an end to the unchristian and impolitic practice of making slaves of the human species in this Province."

In 1774, it had been resolved in a County Convention held in this town, " that we abhor the enslaving of any of the human race, and particularly of the negroes in this country, and that whenever there shall be a door opened, or opportunity presented for anything to be done towards the emancipation of the negroes, we will use our influence and endeavor that such a thing may be brought about."

The new Constitution of 1780, had in its first article declared that "all men are born free and equal."

In 1783, final judgment was given. A citizen was charged with beating and imprisoning a negro servant whom he claimed as his slave. The public would not overlook the offence, and the case was tried and judgment rendered in Worcester. The defendant was found guilty and fined forty shillings. This decision was the downfall of the system. Many who had been in bondage continued as servants in the families of their masters, and the institution died an easy death.*

The preliminary treaty of peace having been signed in November, 1782, and a cessation of hostilities having been proclaimed in the American Army, on the 19th of April, 1783, preparations were made for a proper celebration in this town of the return of peace. The following account is from the "Spy" of May 8, 1783.

"The gentlemen of this town having fixed upon the seventh of this month for a celebration of the return of peace, after an eight years tedious war, a peace honorable to these States as having established us as the first civilized, Independent Empire in this new world,—yesterday morning was ushered in by the ringing of bells, the discharge of 13 cannon, and the display of the American flag. At one o'clock, the gentlemen assembled at the Sun Tavern and dined; after which, a number of sentimental toasts were given, each accompanied by a discharge of cannon. The day was spent with festivity, decency and good order."

The following toasts were given:

1. The American Constellation of Sages that enlighten the world.

2. His Excellency General Washington: May his fame be immortal, as his virtues are unrivalled.

3. The nations of Europe that have been friends to liberty.

4. Love and honor to the blooming Sister States.

5. Happiness to the American heroes that have enfranchised the world.

---
*Barry's History of Massachusetts.

6. Monuments in our breasts to heroes in the bed of honor.

7. May Americans ever act worthy of the liberty they have established, and propagate heroes worthy of their sires.

8. May the Freedom of America with the force of electric fire, give a fatal shock to despotism.

9. May the auspicious dawn of peace conciliate our jarring sentiments, and plant the olive branch in our hearts.

10. Arts and Sciences.

11. Agriculture and Commerce.

12. May the Temple of Virtue reared in America, attract the admiration of mankind.

13. Perpetual Peace, Independence and Happiness to the United States of America.

At sundown, the bells ceased to ring, and thirteen cannon were again discharged. In the evening there was a ball, where the ladies made a brilliant appearance, and heartily joined their expressions of joy on this happy occasion.

A letter was carried in May, from the Committee of Correspondence of the town of Boston, in relation to absentees and refugees. A Committee consisting of Levi Lincoln, William Stearns, Joseph Allen, David Bigelow, Isaiah Thomas, Joseph Wheeler and Jonathan Rice, was appointed to draw up an expression of the sentiment of the town. This committee reported on the 19th of May, and their report was accepted. It was

1. Voted: That this town, with an equal and sacred regard to treaties of peace and alliance; to the Resolves of Congress and the solemn Acts of the Commonwealth, passed from time to time for its preservation, safety and defence, and especially to those great and important principles of Liberty and a Free Government, for which they have been struggling at the risk of their lives, will continue with spirit and firmness, their most vigorous efforts to render glorious, and secure from danger, interruption or diminution, the ends of their past exertions, Peace, Safety and Happiness.

2d. Voted: That this town considers every country, in time of invasion, as having equally right to the assistance, the personal services and property of all its subjects in opposing the assailants,—that this country more than eight years since, was invaded and has been scourged by a war, which for the purpose of reducing it to the servile subjection of foreign domination, has been, by sea and by land, wasting, and by every species of barbarity, distressing its innocent inhabitants; a war that has devastated and burned whole towns, and rendered wretched, and turned out thousands of virtuous Americans, destitute, despoiled and unprovided for by the Treaty of Peace, which leaves them dependent on the gratitude and generosity of their country; a war promoted, encouraged and invited by those, who, the moment the bloody banners were displayed, abandoned their native land, turned parricides, and conspired to involve this country in ruin, tumult and in blood.

3d. Voted: That such traitorous conduct, upon every principle of policy and justice, in all ages and in all countries, would in the opinion of this town, operate a forfeiture of the conspirators' civil and political relations to their injured and betrayed country; cut them off forever, from a standing therein, render them enemies and aliens, and justify those necessary laws, and that general voice of the people, by which they have been thus declared.

4th. Voted: That considering, while the sword was slumbering in its scabbard, when this country was in the hour of quiet, and at peace with the world, only pleading and petitioning for its rights, for a free government, the sentiments of the absentees, their principles, their language and their feelings were fixedly opposed to those rights, and to that freedom, they then preferring, and to evince the sincerity of that preference, engaged to risk their all for its possible attainment, a government totally inconsistent with the principles of the one we have established and for the destruction of which, they have been waging a cruel war; that therefore this town cannot conceive it to be their duty, or their interest, *ever* to provide for the return of such ingrates, to naturalize them, or admit them to the privileges and immunities of citizens.

5th. Voted: That whereas the said absentees and conspirators, have at all times uniformly by their representations, addresses, and avowed principles, considered the subjects of these States, of our great and illustrious ally, and the treaties of alliance, amity and commerce, as the proper subjects of abuse, calumny and reproach, the *former* as the deluded tools of a party spurred on to treason and rebellion; the *second* as the cowardly machines of a Monarch, perfidiously plotting the ruin of the former ; and the latter as originating from the worst of motives, delusive, treacherous, artful, insincere, and not to be adhered to, and have even attempted to seduce the subjects of these States to violate their faith, and those sacred treaties ; That therefore, in the opinion of this town, to admit persons of such principles, and such practices, to incorporate with, and reside among us, would betray the want of a due regard to a generous friend, who has been fighting and bleeding by our side, endanger the treaty and injure our national character.

6th. Voted : That whereas persons of the above description, have been of opinion, which they have been assiduous to propagate, that these States could find happiness or protection, nowhere but in a reunion with the Kingdom of Great Britain ; that left to themselves, they would become the sport of each other, break to pieces and crumble into ruin ; that no calamity was more to be deprecated *for our own sakes* than Independence *established*, and no blessing more earnestly to be sought for than Independence *destroyed ;* And whereas, by a change of British councils, and British measures, there was a prospect of peace, they reprobated that change, and solicited for the purpose above, the continued utmost exertion of British power and British resources, and even after the commencement of the Pacific treaty, with malicious intention, equally hostile to both countries, dared to represent America as the proper subject of an easy conquest ; That therefore, in the opinion of this town, our independence must ever be in danger of annoyance from such persons, who can never have our confidence, friendship or society.

7th. Voted : That the plea for the return of the absentees, of their becoming good subjects, increasing our numbers and our strength, is in the opinion of this town, groundless and fallacious, as it is improbable that persons who have thus acted, that are thus principled and thus situated would, without any new reason, light or argument, alter their conduct, and at once reject those principles they have embraced, and embrace those they have rejected, endeavor to support that government they have been struggling to destroy, cultivate that harmony which they have been industrious to prevent, prevent that discord they have been assiduous to create,—*quell* those *Riots* and *Unlawful Assemblies* which but of late were the foundation of their darling hope,—and endeavor to strengthen that friendship and alliance, which they have labored to weaken, and lied to asperse, and by a conduct the reverse of their past, become useful and good.

8th. Voted: That agreeable to the Treaty of Peace, this town wishes no recollection of past disputes with Great Britain, no repetition of past injuries, but the seeds of discord being excluded, that such a beneficial and satisfactory intercourse may be established between the two countries, as to promise and secure to both, perpetual peace and harmony, which would be extremely difficult, were those persons to reside among us, whom this country considers as the occasion of interrupting that intercourse formerly, and the cause of all their sufferings; especially as these wretched beings have already begun a quarrel with that peace, and those who made it, which terminates a long, bloody and unnatural war.

9th. Voted: That, therefore, in the opinion of this town, it would be extremely dangerous to the peace, the happiness, the liberties, the interest and safety of these States, to suffer persons of the above description to become the subjects of, and to reside in this government, that it would be not only dangerous, but inconsistent with justice, policy, our past laws, the public faith and the principles of a free and independent State, to admit them ourselves, or have them forced upon us, without our consent.

10th. Voted: That in the opinion of this town, this Commonwealth ought with the utmost caution, to naturalize, or in any other way admit as subjects, a common enemy, a set of people, who have been by the united voice of this continent declared outlaws, exiles, aliens, and enemies, dangerous to its political being and happiness.

11th. Voted: That while there are thousands of the innocent, peaceable, defenceless inhabitants of these States, whose property has been destroyed and taken from them in the course of the war, for whom no provision is made, to whom there is no restitution of estates, no compensation for losses, that it would be unreasonable, cruel and unjust, to suffer those who were the wicked occasion of those losses, to obtain a restitution of estates they refused to protect, and which they have abandoned, and forfeited to the justice of their country.

12th. Voted: That whereas, persons of the above description have already made various attempts to introduce themselves into this government, and thereby to establish principles and precedents by which others might be admitted and restored to their forfeited estates; that this town will adopt every reasonable and consistent measure to prevent so great an evil; and that it is their expectation and earnest request of Samuel Curtis, Esq., whom they have chosen to represent them at this critical period, that he will, with firmness and steadiness, continue his patriotic exertions for the above purpose; that he will use his influence to have those good and wholesome laws touching the matter, duly executed, and such others enacted as events and circumstances from time to time may render necessary; that he will receive a copy of the above votes, to the principles of which, the principles of a sovereign and independent government, the principles of our free constitution and those great principles which have carried us triumphantly through a severe and bloody conflict, to these principles he invariably to adhere, and make them the governing rule of his conduct, as what alone under heaven, has given energy to war, will give dignity to peace, and make life happy.

13th. Voted: That it is the expectation of this town, and their earnest request of their Committee of Correspondence, Inspection and Safety, that they will with care and vigilance observe the movements and watch the conduct of our only remaining enemies, that until the further order of government, they will with decision, spirit and firmness, endeavor to enforce and carry into execution, the several laws of this Commonwealth respecting these enemies of our rights, and the rights of mankind; give information should they know of any obtruding themselves into any part of this State, suffer none to remain in this town but caused to be confined immediately for the purpose of transportation according to law, any that may presume to enter it.

The Independence of the States having been acknowledged and Peace declared, the task of reviewing the acts of the town and people of Worcester in the war of the Revolution, ends here. The position which this town assumed and maintained in those trying times, was one to which we of this day may look back with pride.

Although Worcester was at that time a small provincial town, its situation in the heart of the Province, and the fact of its being the shire-town of a large county, enabled it to exert an influence far beyond that indicated by the number of its inhabitants. Responding with readiness to all requisitions for men and means, this town upheld the cause in its darkest hours, and when despondency and gloom prevailed in many portions of the land, and the struggle seemed a hopeless one, no word of discouragement or despair was left for us to record,— save from those who from the beginning were hostile to their country's cause,—but instead, was left a record of hearty coöperation with every measure calculated to secure the Independence of the Colonies.

Out of a total population of a little over 1900, Worcester furnished about 400 soldiers. They were found at Cambridge and Bunker Hill, at Quebec, Long Island, and on the Hudson, at Saratoga, Valley Forge, Monmouth and Yorktown, and on almost every field rendered glorious by noble deeds in behalf of a country struggling for its freedom.

It is a matter of congratulation, that, although differences of opinion existed in the minds of the men of that day, as to the justice or policy of the war, and those differences led to extreme measures in many cases, their descendants inherit no bitterness of feeling, and all are now striving with earnest and honest purpose to perpetuate those institutions which were established through toil, suffering and blood.

APPENDIX.

TOWN OFFICERS FROM 1774 TO 1783.

Town Officers, 1774.

SELECTMEN.

Timothy Paine,
Benjamin Flagg,
Thomas Wheeler,
William Young,
Josiah Pierce.

Clark Chandler, *Town Clerk.*

Hon. John Chandler, *Town Treas.*

COMMITTEE OF CORRESPONDENCE :
William Young,
Timothy Bigelow,
John Smith,
Joshua Bigelow,
David Bancroft,
Jonathan Stone,
Stephen Salisbury.

Town Officers for 1775.

SELECTMEN :

Joshua Bigelow,
Benjamin Flagg,
William Young,
Josiah Pierce,
Jonathan Stone,
Samuel Curtis,
Samuel Miller,

Nathan Baldwin, *Town Clerk.*

Lieut. Nathan Perry, *Town Treas.*

COMMITTEE OF CORRESPONDENCE :
William Young,
Timothy Bigelow,
John Smith,
Joshua Bigelow,
David Bancroft,
Jonathan Stone,
Stephen Salisbury.

Town Officers for 1776.

SELECTMEN :

Benjamin Flagg,
William Young,
Josiah Pierce,
Jonathan Stone,
Samuel Curtis,
Samuel Miller,
David Bigelow.

Nathan Baldwin, *Town Clerk.*

Nathan Perry, *Town Treas.*

COMMITTEE OF CORRESPONDENCE.
Nathan Baldwin,
Nathan Perry,
Asa Moore,
Ezekiel How,
Levi Lincoln.

Town Officers for 1777.

SELECTMEN :

Benjamin Flagg,
William Young,
Nathan Perry,
Jonathan Stone,
David Bigelow,
Benjamin Stowell,
John Kelso.

Nathan Baldwin, *Town Clerk.*

Nathan Perry, *Town Treas.*

COMMITTEE OF CORRESPONDENCE :
John Cunningham,
William Stearns,
Samuel Miller,
Samuel Brown,
Josiah Pierce.

TOWN OFFICERS FOR 1778.

SELECTMEN:

Joshua Bigelow,
Ebenezer Lovell,
Robert Smith,
William Stearns,
Nathaniel Brooks.

William Stearns, *Town Clerk.*

Dr. John Green, *Town Treas.*

COMMITTEE OF CORRESPONDENCE.

Joseph Barber,
Nathaniel Heywood,
Daniel Bigelow,
Jonathan Rice,
William Dana.

TOWN OFFICERS FOR 1779.

SELECTMEN:

William Stearns,
David Bigelow,
Robert Smith,
Nathaniel Brooks,
Thomas Wheeler.

William Stearns, *Town Clerk.*

Dr. John Green, *Town Treas.*

COMMITTEE OF CORRESPONDENCE:

Joseph Barber,
Nathaniel Heywood,
Jonathan Rice,
William Dana,
Jonathan Phillips.

TOWN OFFICERS FOR 1780.

SELECTMEN:

David Bigelow,
Dr. John Green,
Jonathan Rice,
Joseph Barber,
Edward Crafts.

Nathaniel Heywood, *Town Clerk.*

William Gates, *Town Treas.*

COMMITTEE OF CORRESPONDENCE.

Joseph Allen,
Daniel Harris,
David Chadwick,
Thomas Knight,
William Trowbridge.

TOWN OFFICERS FOR 1781.

SELECTMEN:

Samuel Miller,
Nathan Perry,
Wm. McFarland,
Samuel Brown,
John Gleason.

Daniel Goulding, *Town Clerk.*

Nathan Perry, *Town Treas.*

COMMITTEE OF CORRESPONDENCE:

Joseph Allen,
Nathan Baldwin,
Isaiah Thomas.

TOWN OFFICERS FOR 1782.

SELECTMEN:

Samuel Miller,
Nathan Perry,
William McFarland,
Samuel Brown,
John Gleason.

Daniel Goulding, *Town Clerk.*

Nathan Perry, *Town Treas.*

COMMITTEE OF CORRESPONDENCE.

Joseph Allen,
Nathan Baldwin,
Isaiah Thomas.

APPENDIX.] *War of the Revolution.* 117

TOWN OFFICERS FOR 1783.   William G. Maccarty, *Town Clerk.*

SELECTMEN:
Nathan Perry,
Joseph Allen,
Joseph Wheeler,
Samuel Brown,
David Bigelow.

Nathan Perry, *Town Treas.*

COMMITTEE OF CORRESPONDENCE:
Joseph Allen,
Joseph Wheeler,
Isaiah Thomas.

JURY LIST FOR 1776.

Copied from the original in possession of American Antiquarian Society.

The following to serve as Jurors at the Superior Court of Judicature, Court of Assize and General Jail Delivery, namely:

Ezekiel Howe	Ebenezer Lovell	William Young
Noah Jones	Comfort Rice	Timothy Bigelow
Jonathan Stone	Josiah Pierce	Samuel Curtis
David Bigelow	Peter Johnson	Nathan Perry
Thomas Wheeler	William Dana	Nathaniel Moore
James Goodwin	John Fisk	Benjamin Flagg
Samuel Woodburn	Amos Wheeler	John Kelso
Samuel Miller	Jonathan Phillips	David Bancroft
Silas Moore	William Gates	Benjamin Stowell
Stephen Salisbury	Asa Moore	Daniel Bigelow, Jr.

The following to serve as Jurors in the Inferior Court of Common Pleas and Court of General Sessions of the Peace, namely:

Thomas Nichols	Jonathan Lovell	Peter Boyden
Joseph Barber	John Moore	David Thomas
Samuel Brown	Robert Smith	Joseph Sprague
Lemuel Rice	William Taylor	James Moore
Thomas Drury, Jr.	Oliver Curtis	Thomas Beard, Jr.
Jonathan Fiske	James Trowbridge	Samuel Goddard
Ebenezer Wiswall	Solomon Bixby	Ephraim Miller
Samuel McCracken	Jacob Holmes, Jr.	Robert Crawford
Reuben Gray	Robert Gray	Richard Pratt
William McFarland	Josiah Harrington, Jr.	Ebenezer Willington
Moses Miller	John Barber	Joshua Whitney
Daniel Beard	Nathaniel Brooks	Simon Gates
Daniel Harris	Solomon Johnson, Jr.	Joseph Wyley
Thomas Eaton	Benjamin Whitney	Jonathan Gleason
Jonathan Flagg	David Chadwick	Cyprian Stevens
Elisha Gurney	Samuel Clark	Joseph Miller
James Barber	Joseph Hastings	Asa Ward
William Johnson	Levi Houghton	Samuel Bridge
Isaac Willard	John Nazro	John Smith
Jonas Nichols		

LIST OF VOTERS FOR MARCH MEETING, 1775,

Qualified according to the Last List of Estates by which the Taxes are made:

Charles Adams
Nath'l Adams
Joshua Bigelow
Daniel Bigelow, Jr.
Samuel Bridge
Timothy Bigelow
Samuel Brown
James Brown
Luke Brown
Joseph Blair
James Barber
David Bigelow
Samuel Brooks
John Barber
Thomas Brown
Jona Bartlett
Joseph Barber
Nathaniel Brooks
Daniel Beard
John Beard
Isaac Barnard, Esq.
Solomon Bixby
John Barnard
John Chandler, Esq.
Benjamin Chapin
David Chadwick
Joseph Clark
Robert Crawford
Samuel Curtis
Rufus Chandler
Jonas Cutting
Gardner Chandler
John Curtis
Jacob Chamberlain
  do as Guardian to
    Daniel Heywood
William Cowdin
Sarah Chandler
John Chamberlain
Clark Chandler
Samuel Clark
———— Chamberlain
Edward Crafts
Francis Cutting
Joseph Dwelle
Andrew Duncan
William Campbell
Elijah Dix
William Dana
William Elder
John Elder
Samuel Eaton
Benjamin Flagg
John Tufts
Jona. Tufts
David Fish

Jonah Flagg
Rufus Flagg
Elisha Gurney
Palmer Goulding
John Green
William Gates
John Gates
Jona. Gates
James Goodwin
Samuel Goddard
Reuben Gray
Isaac Gleason
Reuben Gleason
Jonas Gleason
Robert Gray
Simon Gates
Jona. Grout
John Griggs
Phinehas Gleason
Josiah Harrington
Jacob Holmes
Jacob Holmes, Jr.
Francis Harrington
Joseph Hastings
Ebenezer Holbrook, Jr.
Jacob Hemmenway
Ezekiel How
William Harris
Jonas Hubbard
Noah Harris
Nathaniel Healey
Phinehas Heywood
Josiah Harrington, Jr.
Levi Houghton
Noah Jones
Sol. Johnson
Micah Johnson
Peter Johnson
Israel Jennison
William Jones
Edward Knight
Thomas Knight
John Kelso
Paul Kingsbury
Josiah Knight
Daniel Knight
Ebenezer Lovell
Jonathan Lovell
Nathaniel Moore
William Mahon
Silas Moore
Asa Moore
John Mower
William Mahon
James McFarland
William McFarland

Samuel Miller
John Moore
Samuel McCracken
David Moore
Ephraim Miller
James Moore
Moses Miller
Samuel Mower
Samuel Mower, Jr.
Samuel Moore
Joseph Miller
Thomas Nichols
John Nazro
Jona. Orland
Timothy Paine, Esq.
William Paine
James Putnam, Esq.
Jona. Phillips
Nathan Perry
Richard Pratt
Josiah Pierce
Nathan Patch
James Quigley
Abraham Rice
Jonathan Rice
Thomas Rice
Tyrus Rice
David Richardson
Zeb. Rice
Lemuel Rice
John Stearns
Benjamin Stowell
Cornelius Stowell
Mary Stearns
Elisha Smith
Elisha Smith, Jr.
Robert Smith
Ab. Smith
Cyprian Stevens
William Jennison Stearns
John Smith, 2d.
Stephen Salisbury
Joseph Sprague
Othniel Taylor
William Taylor
James Trowbridge
Jabez Tatman
David Thomas
Nahum Willard
James Willard
Ebenezer Wiswall
Levi Newton
Joshua Whitney
Amos Wheeler
Ebenezer Willington
Joseph Wiley

Benjamin Whitney	William Young	James Hart, Jr.
Benj. Whitney, Jr.	Daniel Boyden	Jonas Nichols
Mary Walker	Darius Boyden	Gershom Rice
Samuel Whitney	David Bancroft	Comfort Rice
John Walker	Thomas Beard	Jonathan Stone
Ebenezer White	Thomas Beard, Jr.	Jacob Stevens
Adam Walker	Peter Boyden	Gershom Rice, Jr.
Asa Ward	William Bancroft	Thomas Drury
Samuel Woodburn	Oliver Curtis	Thomas Drury, Jr.

This List is copied from the original List, certified by Timothy Paine, Josiah Pierce, Benj. Flagg—Selectmen, in possession of American Antiquarian Society.

ROLL OF CAPT. TIMOTHY BIGELOW'S COMPANY,

in the Colony Service, on the Alarm of April 19, 1775.

Timothy Bigelow, Captain.
Jonas Hubbard, 1st Lieut.
John Smith, 2d   "
William Gates,   Sergeant.
Nathaniel Harrington,   "
John Kanady,   "
William Dana,   "
John Pierce,   Corporal.
Cyprian Stevens,   "
Joel Smith,   "
Nathaniel Heywood, "
Eli Putnam, Drummer.
John Hair, Fifer.
Joseph Pierce, "
Peter Boyden,   Private.
Benjamin Bennett,   "
David Chadwick,   "
Eli Chapin,   "
Philip Donehue,   "
Benjamin Estabrook, "
Josiah Flagg,   "
Phinehas Flagg,   "
Nathaniel Flagg,   "
Josiah Gates,   "
Thomas Gates,   "
Jonathan Gleason,   "
William Griggs,   "
Edward Hair,   "
Asa Harrington,   "
John Hall,   "
Artemas Knight,   "
John Knower   "
Ephraim Miller,   "
William Miles,   "
Joseph Morse,   "
Jonas Nichols,   "
Solomon Smith,   "
Phinehas Ward,   "
Ebenezer Wiswall,   "

Josiah Pierce,   Private.
James Wiser,   "
Daniel Haven,   "
William Trowbridge, "
John Cole,   "
Joseph Ball,   "
Jonathan Stone,   "
Samuel Wesson,   "
Thomas Nichols,   "
Thomas Knight,   "
Samuel Harrington,   "
Thomas Lynde,   "
Joseph Cunningham,   "
Robert Crawford,   "
Moses Hamilton,   "
Samuel Bennett,   "
Samuel Hemmenway,   "
William Walker,   "
Nicholas Powers,   "
Daniel Wellington,   "
William Curtis,   "
William Treadwell,   "
Edward Swan,   "
Joseph Curtis,   "
Samuel Cook,   "
Samuel Duncan,   "
Asa Ward,   "
Elisha Fuller,   "
John Totman,   "
Joseph Thorp,   "
George Walker,   "
Thomas Drury,   "
Samuel Brown,   "
Adam Hemmenway,   "
James Taylor,   "
Joseph Miller,   "
Josiah Perry,   "

ROLL OF CAPT. BENJAMIN FLAGG'S COMPANY,

in the Colony Service on the Alarm of April 19, 1775.

Benjamin Flagg,	Captain.	Daniel Stearns,	Private.
William McFarland,	Lieut.	Edward Crafts,	"
Ebenezer Lovell,	Ensign.	Samuel Gates,	"
Daniel Beard,	Serg't.	David Richards,	"
Benjamin Flagg, Jr.,	"	Gershom Holmes,	"
Eleazer Holbrook,	Private.	Simon Gates,	"
Isaac Morse,	"	Isaac Knight,	"
Abel Holbrook,	"	Ezekiel Howe, Jr.,	"
Jacob Holmes, Jr.	"	Abel Flagg,	"
Simeon Duncan,	"	Levi Houghton,	"
Samuel Ward,	"	Samuel Whitney,	"
Eleazer Hawes,	"	Benjamin Whitney, Jr.,	"
Isaac Gleason,	"	Josiah Harrington,	"
Robert Smith,	"	Jonathan Stone,	"
Samuel Sturtevant,	"	Samuel Miller, Jr.,	"
Oliver Pierce,	"		

ROLL OF COMPANY FROM WORCESTER,

Under Capt. Jonas Hubbard.

	Enlisted,		Enlisted,
Jonas Hubbard, Capt.,	April 24.	John Knower, Private,	April 24.
John Smith, 1st Lieut.	"	Artemas Knight, "	"
William Gates, 2d "	"	Ephraim Miller, "	"
Nathaniel Harrington, Serg't.	"	William Miles, "	"
John Kanady,	" "	Joseph Morse, "	"
John Pierce,	" "	Jonas Nichols, "	"
Cyprian Stevens,	" "	Josiah Pierce, "	"
Joel Smith, Corporal,	April 25.	Solomon Smith, "	"
Nathaniel Heywood, "	" 24.	Ithamer Smith, "	"
Jonathan Stone, "	"	Phinehas Ward, "	"
Samuel Wesson, "	"	Ebenezer Wiswall, "	"
Joseph Ball, Drummer,	"	James Wiser, "	"
John Hair, Fifer,	"	Daniel Haven, "	"
Joseph Pierce, "	"	William Trowbridge, "	June 7.
Peter Boyden, Private,	"	Eli Putnam, "	"
Benjamin Bennett, "	"	John Cole, "	June 6.
David Chadwick, "	"	Daniel Gale, "	May 1.
Eli Chapin, "	"	Samuel Gates, "	Apr. 25.
Philip Donehue, "	"	Simon Gates, "	"
Benjamin Estabrook, "	"	Simon Crosby, "	May 1.
Josiah Flagg, "	"	Uriah Eaton, "	" 3.
Phinehas Flagg, "	"	John McGuire, "	" 1.
Nathaniel Flagg, "	"	Silas Henry, "	" 1.
Josiah Gates, "	"	Gershom Holmes, "	Apr. 25.
Thomas Gates, "	"	Elijah Hawes, "	"
Jonathan Gleason, "	"	Isaac Jones, "	May 3.
William Griggs, "	"	Thomas Nichols, "	Apr. 26.
Gideon Griggs, "	"	David Richards, "	" 25.
Edward Hair, "	"	Richard Stowers, "	" "
Asa Harrington, "	"	Ebenezer Ephraim, "	May 1.
John Hall, "	"	Jonas Clark, "	"

This Roll is dated Aug. 1, 1775. These men served 3 months and 15 days.

LIST OF MEN IN COL. THOMAS CRAFT'S REGIMENT OF ARTILLERY, 1775.

Edward Crafts,	Captain.	William Treadwell, 2d "
Nath'l Nazro,	Capt. Lieut.	William Trowbridge, Private.
William Dana,	1st Lieut.	

ALL FROM WORCESTER IN OTHER COMPANIES, 1775.

Names.	Rank.	Regiment.	Captain.
Timothy Bigelow,	Major,	Col. Jona. Ward's.	
Samuel Fairfield,	Private,	"	Seth Washburne.
Samuel Brown,	1st Lieut,	"	Josiah Fay.
Daniel Johnson,	Corporal,	"	"
Reuben Bancroft,	Private,	"	"
William Stearns,	"	"	"
Asa Stearns,	"	"	"
William Stearns,	"	"	"
Titus Smith,	"	"	"
Robert Jennison,	"	"	"
Samuel Stearns, Jr,	"	Col. Eph. Doolittle,	John Jones,
Isaac Cutting,	"	"	"
Phinehas Smith,	"	"	"
Joseph Thorp,	"	Col. John Nixon,	Wm. Smith.
Edward Conner,	"	"	Joseph Bullen.
Phinehas Smith,	"	Col. Eph. Doolittle,	John Jones.
Samuel Stearns,	"	"	"
Isaac Cutting,	"	"	"

ROLL OF CAPT. WILLIAM GATES' COMPANY,

In Col. Jonathan Holman's Regiment in Chelsea Camp, New York, Sept. 4, 1776.

William Gates,	Captain.	Samuel Gates,	Private.
Nathaniel Heywood,	2d Lieut.	Silas Gates,	"
*Jonas Nichols,	Sergeant.	Vernon Gleason,	"
Phinehas Flagg,	"	Joshua Harrington,	"
Reuben Rice,	"	Samuel Hemmenway,	"
Benjamin Chapin,	Corporal.	Silas Henry,	"
Josiah Flagg,	"	Isaac Kingman,	"
Ebenezer Wiswall,	"	Daniel Moore,	"
Thomas Gates,	"	John McGuire,	"
Gideon Griggs,	Drummer.	*William Kenney,	"
*Joseph Boyden,	Private.	Daniel Stowell,	"
*Jonathan Bancroft,	"	Daniel Stearns,	"
Benjamin Cutting,	"	Noah Sturtevant,	"
Daniel Chadwick,	"	Peter Slater,	"
James Case,	"	Solomon Smith,	"
Isaac Cutting,	"	William Harris,	"
Nathan Cutler,	"	William Stearns,	"
Zebulon Cutting,	"	*William Stone,	"
Elisha Dunham,	"	William Stowell,	"
Richard Draper,	"	James Taylor,	"
Simeon Duncan,	"	*Thomas Severy,	"
Benjamin Flagg,	"	Moses Wilder,	"

*Men from the South Parish, now Auburn.

Elisha Fuller,	Private.	Phinehas Rice,	Private.
Daniel Gale,	"	Phinehas Smith,	"
Noah Gale,	"	Reuben Gleason,	"
Paul Gates,	"	William Knight,	"
Phinehas Gleason,	"		

MEN FROM WORCESTER IN COL. THOMAS CRAFT'S REGIMENT OF ARTILLERY, 1776.

	Rank.	Captain.
Edward Clarke Weld,	Matross,	Thomas Melville.
James Kennedy,	"	"
Elisha Smith,	"	James Swan.
Uriah Eaton,	"	"
David Gleason,	"	"
Talman Allen,	"	"
Nathan Johnson,	"	"
Samuel Furbush,	"	William Todd.
Ebenezer Hastings,	5th Gunner	"
Daniel Baird,	Sergeant.	"
Titus Smith,	Fifer,	"
William Harrington,	Bombardier,	"
Noah Harrington,	Matross,	"
William Griggs,	"	"
Samuel Griggs,	"	"
John Gray,	"	Winthrop Gray.
Joseph Thorp.	Sergeant,	David Henshaw.
Samuel Duncan,	"	"
Edward Hair,	Corporal,	"
William Shiel,	Bombardier,	"
Jacob Smith,	Matross,	"
Elisha Clark,	"	"
David Clark,	"	"
Jedediah Healy.	"	"

LIST OF MEN IN COL. THOMAS CRAFT'S REGIMENT OF ARTILLERY, 1777.

	Rank.	Company.
Job Weeden,	Corporal,	Capt. John Balch.
James Swan,	Major,	
Simon Crosby,	Matross,	1st. Company.
Nathaniel Nazro,	Capt. Lieut.	Capt. David Henshaw.
Samuel Duncan,	Sergeant,	"
Edward Hair,	"	"
Eben. Hastings,	Bombardier,	"
Simeon Duncan,	"	"
David Clark,	Gunner,	"
Elisha Clark,	"	"
John Hair,	Fifer,	"
Jedediah Healy,	Matross,	"
Jacob Smith,	"	"
Titus Smith,	Fifer,	Capt. William Todd
William Harrington,	Gunner,	"
James Furbush,	Matross,	"
Noah Harrington,	"	"

Samuel Griggs,	Matross,	Capt. William Todd.
William Griggs,	"	"
Edward Clarke Weld,	Gunner,	Capt. Thomas Melville.
Alexander Wilson,	Filer,	"
James Kennedy,	Matross,	"

ROLL OF CAPT. DAVID CHADWICK'S COMPANY,

That marched to Hadley on an alarm at Bennington, under command of Lieut. Col. Benjamin Flagg, by desire of Brigadier General Warner, Aug. 28, 1777.

Benjamin Flagg,	Lieut. Col.	Phinehas Gleason,	Private.
David Chadwick,	Captain.	John Goodwin,	"
Abel Holbrook,	Lieut.	Joseph Gray,	"
Jonathan Stone,	"	Stephen Gates,	"
Nathaniel Brooks,	Sergeant.	James Gates,	"
James Moore,	"	Joseph Gleason,	"
Josiah Harrington,	"	Peter Jennison,	"
Phinehas Jones,	"	Daniel Jennison,	"
Josiah Flagg,	Corporal.	Daniel Heywood,	"
John Moore,	"	Samuel Hemmenway,	"
Joseph Ball,	Private.	Joel Howe,	"
William Buxton,	"	Daniel Harris,	"
Daniel Beard,	"	Silas Harrington,	"
Jonas Bancroft,	"	Joshua Harrington,	"
Jonas Bancroft 2d,	"	Jacob Holmes,	"
Jona. Bancroft,	"	Peter Hardy,	"
Benjamin Bancroft,	"	Edward Knight,	"
Gershom Bigelow, Jr.,	"	Hugh Kelso,	"
Timothy Barber,	"	John Moore,	"
Isaac Chadwick,	"	Samuel McCracken,	"
John Crowle,	"	William McFarland,	"
Elisha Clark.	"	Thomas Nichols,	"
Elisha Crosby,	"	John Noyes,	"
Timothy Carter,	"	Josiah Perry,	"
Jonathan Cutter,	"	Jona. Phillips,	"
Wilson Chamberlain,	"	Josiah Phillips,	"
Oliver Curtis,	"	Nathan Patch,	"
Eli Chapin,	"	Lemuel Rice,	"
Benjamin Carter,	"	David Richards,	"
Simeon Duncan,	"	Josiah Rice,	"
Simeon Duncan, Jr.	"	Robert Smith,	"
Thomas Eaton,	"	William Snow, Jr.,	"
John Elder,	"	John Taylor,	"
Nathaniel Flagg,	"	Joseph Thorp,	"
Samuel Gates,	"	Samuel Wiley,	"
Jacob Works,	"	William Young,	"
Samuel Brown,	Adjutant.		

NINE MONTHS' MEN,

Raised agreeably to Resolve of General Court, April 20, 1778.

Thomas Betterly,
John Warren,
William Betterly,
Samuel Newton,
Reuben Rice,
Joseph Ball,
Benjamin Flagg,
Amos Johnson.

The above were drafted for service on the Hudson river.

MEN FROM WORCESTER IN CONTINENTAL SERVICE IN 1778.

Thomas Betterly
John Warren
William Betterly
Samuel Newton
Reuben Rice

Joseph Ball
Samuel Gates
Elisha Crosby
Joseph Gray
William Gates

Samuel Hemmenway
Amos Johnson
Edward Swan
Richard Draper

NINE MONTHS' MEN, DRAFTED IN 1779.

John Hair,   Capt. Lovell's Co.
Edward Hair,   "   "
Thomas Gleason,   "   "
Aaron Stone,   "   "
Reuben Wyman,   "   "
Dick Richards,   "   "
Samuel Johnson,   "   "

Samuel Whitney,   Capt. Whitney's Co.
Elisha Crosby,   "   "
Benj. Cutting,   "   "
Jacob Nash,   "   "
Paul Gates,   "   "
William Mattell,   "   "

LIST OF SIX MONTHS' MEN
Raised agreeably to Resolve of June, 1780.

Benjamin Russell,
Reuben Wilder,
Amos Smith,
Elisha Dunham,
George Filmore,
Reuben Hubbard,
Samuel Mellan,
Jacob Nash,

Daniel Wiswall,
Samuel Jones,
Asa Gates,
Jacob Gurney,
Bela Noyes,
Jeffrey Hemmenway,
Levi Hubbard.

LIST OF MEN FROM WORCESTER, 1780.
Returned Dec. 27, 1781.

Amos Smith
Elisha Dunham
George Filmore
Samuel Mahan
Reuben Hubbard

Asa Gates
Samuel Jones
Bela Noyes
Jacob Nash
Daniel Wiswall

Benjamin Russell
Jacob Gurney
Reuben Wyman
Jeffrey Hemmenway
Levi Hubbard

SIX MONTHS' MEN FROM WORCESTER IN 1780.

Elisha Dunham
George Philmore
Reuben Hubbard
Samuel Mahan

Jacob Nash
Daniel Wiswall
Samuel Jones
Asa Gates

Jacob Gurney
Bela Noyes
Jeffrey Hemmenway
Levi Hubbard

Resolves of Dec. 2.

Ebenezer Marsh
Robert Booth
John Edmunds
Francis Harris
Israel Barrett
Benjamin Johnson
William McConkey

Jupiter—negro
John Spring
Cato
John Hinds
Ebenezer Fiske
Abiah Warren
John Gleason

Elmer Jordan
Thomas Gleason
Joseph Reed
Joseph Dwelle
Reuben Wyman
Thomas Morse
George Filmore

MEM. FROM ARMY BOOKS, 1780.

	Rank.	Regiment.		Rank.	Regiment.
Francis Savage,	Corp.	Col. Bigelow's	William Bacon,	Pr.	Col. Bigelow's
Richard Williams,	Pr.	"	Uriah Johnson,	"	"
John Lane,	"	"	Silas Whitney,	"	"
John Knower,	Serg't	"	Simon Glasco,	"	"
John Bradley,	Pr.	"	Ebenezer Whitney,	"	"
Cato Dawes,	"	"	Samuel Ball,	"	"
John Johnson,	"	"	Robert Cook,	"	"
John Avis,	"	"	Seth Partridge,	Corp.	"

MEMORANDUM FROM ARMY BOOKS IN LAND OFFICE.

INFANTRY.

	Rank.	Company.	Regiment.				
John Annisimug,		Capt. Hunt's	Col. Vose's	Dec. 4,	1778	Dec. 31,	1779.
James Quigley,		" Oliver's	" Graton's	Feb. 10,	1777.	June 5,	1779.
Pomp Benglasesses,		"	"	" 6,	"	July 22,	1777.
Thomas Wesson,		" Smith's	Col. Bigelow's	Aug. 19,	"	Dec. 31,	1779.
Samuel Priest,		"	"	Oct. 1,	"		
Joseph Pierce,	Q'r M'r S'g't	" Pierce's	"	March 19,	"	March 31,	"
John Knower,	Sergeant,	"	"	July 14,	"	Dec. 31,	"
Uriah Johnson,	Drummer,	"	"	" 4,	"		
Cuff Annum,	Private,	"	"	March 25,	"	Apr. 19,	"
John Bradley,	"	"	"	" 31,	"	Dec. 31,	"
Simon Glasco,	"	"	"	May 23,	"	"	"
John Avis,	"	"	"	March 31,	"	"	"
William Bacon,	"	"	"	"	"	"	"
Cato Dawes,	"	"	"	March 27,	"	"	"
Samuel Ball,	"	"	"	May 17,	"	July 9,	"
William Waters,	"	"	"	Aug 20,	"	Dec 31,	"
Ebenezer Whitney,	"	"	"	Sept. 14,	"		
Richard Draper,	"	"	"	" 2,	"	Jan. 31,	1778.
William Cowdin,	"	"	"	May 6,	"	Oct. 21,	1777.
James Lanman,	"	"	"	March 31,	"	Jan. 1,	1778.
John Johnson,	"	Capt. Brown's	"	Apr. 15,	"	Dec. 31,	1779.
Francis Savage,	"	" Martin's	"	March 10,			

ARTILLERY.

William Miles,	Corporal,	Capt. Treadwell's	Col. Crane's	June 21,	1777.	Dec 31,	1779.
Peter Slater,	Matross,	"	"	April 6,	"	"	"
Nathan Johnson,	"	"	"	"	"	"	"
John Hunter,	"	"	"	May 7,	"	"	"
Aaron Smith,	"	"	"	June 12,	"	"	"
Daniel Johnson,	"	"	"	April 10,	"	Sept 11,	1777
John Fowle,	"	"	"	Jan'y 10,	"	Oct. 7,	"
Elisha Dunham,	"	"	"	May 31,	"	Dec. 31,	"
Edward Swan,	"	"	"	"	1778.	Oct. 21,	1779.
John Thompson,	Charlton"	"	"	April 18,	1777.	" 31,	"
Richard Barnard,	Private,		Col Marshall's	Dec. 9,	1779.	Dec. 31,	"
Isaac Johns,	"	"	" Sprout's	July 1,	"	"	"
Joseph Gamble,	"	"	" Putnam's	April 12,	1777.	"	"
Thomas Taylor,	"	"	"	Jan. 1,	1777.	July 5,	1777.
Uriah Eaton,	Sergeant,	Capt. Holden's	" Nixon's	March 1,	"	Dec. 31,	1779.
Solomon Smith,	"	"	"	April 1,	"	July 5,	1777.
Elisha Gill, for Leicester,	"	Capt. Brown's	" Jackson's	Jan. 10,	1777.		
Simon Crosby,	"	"	" Sheldon's	Jan. 1,	1780.	Aug 1,	1780.
Lemuel Longley,	"	"	" Lamb's Lt. Art.	"	"	Mar. 16,	"

These Lists of Men in the Service, are taken from manuscripts of the late WILLIAM LINCOLN, in possession of the American Antiquarian Society.

Quaint Advertizements of the Period.

TO BE SOLD.

BY John Nazro at his store in Worcester, West India and New England Rum, Wine, Brandy, Geneva, Jamaica Spirit, Loaf and Brown Sugar, Raisins, choice, French and Spanish Indigo, Cake Soap, Pimento, Otter, Madder, Coffee, Salt Fish, Flour, &c., &c.
(Spy, Aug. 16, 1775.)

TO BE SOLD.

BY William Hubbard & Nathaniel Prentice Peabody, at their Store in Worcester, near the Meeting-house, the following Articles for *money only*: viz: West India and New England Rum, by the Hogshead or Barrel, Geneva by the Case; different Qualities of Brown Sugar by the Hogshead, Barrel, Hundred, or Single Pound; good French Indigo by the Dozen, Pound or Ounce; Molasses by the Hogshead, choice Coffee by the Pound, Dozen, Hundred or Thousand Weight; a few squares of 7 by 9 Window Glass; a few Pieces of Coarse Broad Cloth by retail; German Serges, Shalloons and Tammies by Retail; also Crimson Broad Cloth and Crimson everlasting suitable for Women's Cloaks; Red Half-Thicks by the yard, and good Writing Paper by the Quire.
(Spy, Sept. 29, 1775.)

I. THOMAS, the late publisher of this paper, is very sorry that so many of his customers are so unkind as to neglect paying him the several small sums due to him for services already performed. He has made several journeys to Worcester to receive his just dues, but to his surprise finds the old proverb verified, "out of Sight, out of Mind." He once more earnestly begs that those who are indebted to him for Newspapers, &c., (if it is but two pence,) would immediately pay their respective balances to Mr. Daniel Bigelow, Jr., one of the publishers, as so many small sums when collected together will be of essential service, and the want of which will be a great detriment to ISAIAH THOMAS.
Boston, July 22, 1776.
(Spy, July 24, 1776.)

ALL persons indebted to John Nazro, either by bond, note or book, are earnestly desired without delay to call at his store and make payment thereof to said Nazro; the present situation of affairs, and the still darker prospect, being sufficient to influence every honest man to have nothing of that nature undone that can be done.
(Spy, Aug. 7, 1776.)

TAKEN UP. A red Cow, supposed to be 6 years old, with a White Tail and Belly and some in her Forehead, branded on the left Horn, and half crop on her left Ear. The owner may have her again by paying charges and applying to JONATHAN LOVELL.
(Spy, Nov. 27, 1776.)

TO BE SOLD.

A SPRIGHTLY, healthy Negro Wench, 20 years of age, born in the Country, and can do any kind of housework. She will be a valuable servant in a Country tavern, as she has lived in one several years.

Enquire of the Printer.

(Spy, Dec. 11, 1776.)

TO BE SOLD.

A VERY likely negro man about twenty-one years of age, has had the small pox, and well understands the farming business.

Enquire of the Printer.

(Spy, Feb. 20, 1777.)

FLAX SEED. Six shillings per bushel given for Good Merchantable Flax Seed, by Elijah Dix, at his Store in Worcester. The crop of Flax being very great this year, the preserving of the Seed will be a great service to the State. It is to be hoped that a regard for the interests of America and a handsome price for the seed will be a sufficient inducement to those who have any to part with. It is collected for the public service only.

(Spy, Sept. 4, 1777.)

ADVERTIZEMENT EXTRAORDINARY!

MADE their Escape from the custody of the Subscriber, on the night of the twenty-fifth, two Barrels of Sugar; supposed to be inimical to all Sourness. Said Sugar is of a dark complexion, and about Four Hundred Weight in Quantity. Whoever will apprehend said Sugar and imprison it or otherwise secure it so that the subscriber may have it again, shall be entitled to a reward of four Guineas and all necessary charges paid by me.

LEWIS ALLEN.

(Spy, Feb. 5, 1778.)

HEART AND CLUB GERMAN STEEL.

A QUANTITY of Genuine Heart and Club German Steel may be had at Samuel & Stephen Salisbury's Store in Worcester, if applied for soon. Also, a Quantity of Bar Iron, English Steel, Choice Brandy, New England and West India Rum, Brown Sugar, Coffee, Chocolate, Raisins, Rice, Ginger, Pepper, Allspice, Redwood, Logwood, Alum, Copperas, Brimstone, Powder and Shot, &c.

(Spy, Feb. 19, 1778.)

TAKEN UP. A few days ago, between the Meeting-house in Worcester and the Meeting-house in Leicester, a certain matter or thing, which the connoisseurs in Female head-dressing term a cushing, but probably it might be designed for some other purpose. It has something of an appearance like a wig, but if it is a wig, it is a female one; this mass has been penetrated, and its inward part found to be woolly, the top part of it framed with iron, and its outward coat hairy and rough. The iron, wool and hair of which this curious machine is chiefly composed is supposed to be worth considerable. The person who has lost it, proving her or his property, and paying charges, may have it again by applying at the Printing Office.

(Spy, Nov. 18, 1779.)

TO BE SOLD.

A LIKELY Negro Woman, about 30 years of age, understands all kinds of household work, and is an excellent Cook.
(Spy, Aug. 13, 1778.)   Enquire of the Printer.

NOTICE IS HEREBY GIVEN to all aspiring heroes, who have a spirit above slavery and trade, and are willing to become Gentlemen Soldiers by bearing arms in the 5th Massachusetts Regiment of foot in the service of the United States of America, that by repairing to Ensign Benjamin Gilbert, of Brookfield, they will be kindly entertained as recruits; shall enter into present pay and good quarters, and when they join the regiment, shall receive new clothes, arms and accoutrements, and everything else to complete a gentleman soldier.   RUFUS PUTNAM, Col.
Brookfield, April 21, 1780.
(Spy, April 27, 1780.)

PRICES OF PEWS IN MEETING HOUSE, 1763.

No. 1—£8.	No. 21—£5 10s.	No. 42—£7 10s.
" 2—£9.	" 22—£6 13s.	" 43—£7 10s.
" 3—£8.	" 23—£6 12s.	" 44—£8.
" 4—£4 10s.	" 24—£6 12s.	" 45—£8.
" 5—£5.	" 25—£5 10s.	" 46—£8.
" 6—£6.	" 26—£6 12s.	" 47—£8.
" 7—£6 12s.	" 27—£6 12s.	" 48—£6.
" 8—£6 12s.	" 28—£6.	" 49—£6.
" 9—£5 10s.	" 29—£5.	" 50—£——.
" 10—£6 12s.	" 30—£4 10s.	" 51—£8.
" 11—£6 12s.	" 31—£8.	" 52—£7 10s.
" 12—£6 12s.	" 32—£9.	" 53—£7 10s.
" 13—£5 10s.	" 33—£8.	" 54—£5 15s.
" 14—£8.	" 34—£6 10s.	" 55—£5 5s.
" 15—£9.	" 35—£5 15s.	" 56—£5 5s.
" 16—£9.	" 36—£5 15s.	" 57—£6.
" 17—£7.	" 37—£5 15s.	" 58—£5 10s.
" 18—£9.	" 38—£6.	" 59—£5 15s.
" 19—£9.	" 39—£5 5s.	" 60—£5 15s.
" 20—£8.	" 40—£5 5s.	" 61—£6.
	" 41—£5 15s.	

www.ingramcontent.com/pod-product-compliance
Lightning Source LLC
Chambersburg PA
CBHW020110170426
43199CB00009B/477